Empire of
ALEXANDER THE GREAT

Alexander's Route

miles   100   400

km   100   400

ARAL
SEA

SCYTHIA

• Alexandria Eschiate

• Samarkand

N SEA

MEDIA

PARTHIA

cbatana

Alex
Ari
(H

Khyber
Pass

Bucephala

R. Hydaspes

Sangala

R. Beas

Alexandria
Prophthasia

A

n

INDIA

usa

PERSIA

Opiana •

Persepolis

GEDROSIA

Indus R.

PERSIAN GULF

• Pura

MEKRAN

ARABIAN SEA

ALEXANDER THE GREAT

Alexander the Great

Alexander continually had coins and medals made, and it is from these, scattered all over the antique world, and discovered by accident or dug up in later centuries, that we know how he looked.

ALEXANDER
THE GREAT

JOHN GUNTHER

STERLING PUBLISHING CO., INC.
New York

A FLYING POINT PRESS BOOK

Design: PlutoMedia
Front cover painting: The Battle of Alexander against King Darius,
by Pietro da Cortona.
Photo credit: Erich Lessing/Art Resource, NY
Frontispiece: The British Museum

Library of Congress Cataloging-in-Publication Data

Gunther, John, 1901-1970.
Alexander the Great / John Gunther. -- Updated ed.
p. cm. -- (Sterling point books)
Originally published: New York : Random House, 1953.
Includes index.
ISBN-13: 978-1-4027-4519-5 (trade)
ISBN-10: 1-4027-4519-2
ISBN-13: 978-1-4027- 4139-5 (pbk.)
ISBN-10: 1-4027- 4139-1
1. Alexander, the Great, 356-323 B.C.--Juvenile literature. 2. Greece--History--Macedonian expansion, 359-323 B.C.--Juvenile literature. 3. Greece--Kings and rulers--Biography--Juvenile literature. 4. Generals--Greece--Biography--Juvenile literature. I. Title.

DF234.25.G8 2006
938′.07092--dc22
[B]
2006032133

1 3 5 7 9 10 8 6 4 2

Published by Sterling Publishing Co., Inc.
387 Park Avenue South, New York, NY 10016
Original edition published by Random House, Inc.
Copyright © 1953 by John Gunther
New material in this updated edition
Copyright © 2007 by Flying Point Press
Map copyright © by Richard Thompson, Creative Freelancers, Inc.
Distributed in Canada by Sterling Publishing
c/o Canadian Manda Group, 165 Dufferin Street
Toronto, Ontario, Canada M6K 3H6
Distributed in the United Kingdom by GMC Distribution Services
Castle Place, 166 High Street, Lewes, East Sussex, England BN7 1XU
Distributed in Australia by Capricorn Link (Australia) Pty. Ltd.
P.O. Box 704, Windsor, NSW 2756, Australia

For information about custom editions, special sales, premium and
corporate purchases, please contact Sterling Special Sales
Department at 800-805-5489 or specialsales@sterlingpub.com.

CONTENTS

Part One

Part Two

CONTENTS

Part Three

ALEXANDER THE GREAT

PART ONE

CHAPTER 1

THE BOY AND THE GIANT HORSE

THE BOY STOOD OUT THERE IN THE HOT SUN. He was of medium height, with ruddy blond hair, a straight nose, blue eyes, and a handsome figure. He had great physical courage and energy, and his mind was packed with dreams—such dreams as few people have ever had. His name was Alexander, and he was the son of Philip, King of Macedon.

The boy waited out in the sunshine, watching.

Soon there was a commotion, and Alexander saw his father, Philip, approach. Philip was a powerful, burly man, who was blind in one eye and walked with a limp. The boy was fond of him.

The sun is very hot in Greece and Macedonia in April. Alexander, who was about fourteen, and who loved to watch everything that went on around the palace, squinted up at the burning sun.

King Philip saw Alexander across the courtyard, and waved to him cheerfully. Surrounding Philip were courtiers, attendants, and horsemen. The Macedonians could ride like demons; they were practically centaurs.

The town where this took place was called Pella, and it was the capital of Macedonia. Really it was not a town at all, in our sense, but a mountain village—consisting mostly of stone huts, barracks for the fierce soldiery, and temples. There were multitudes of gods in those days, and people took them seriously, which is why so many temples were always being built.

The time was about 342 B.C., some three hundred years before Jesus Christ was born. That may seem a very long time ago, but from the point of view of historical time it is not long at all. In fact, if you count it up in terms of human lifetimes, it is only about seventy generations ago.

King Philip's scouts had just returned from a foray into the neighboring hills, and they had bought some horses in the market. One after another these new horses were galloped around in the courtyard, while Philip, with his expert eye, looked them over.

Alexander, fascinated by the excitement of this spectacle and the beauty of the horses, watched eagerly from across the court. He got up on a fence to see better. None of the horses had ever been saddled before, and even the hard-riding Macedonian cavalrymen found them hard to mount and break in.

Then a horse was brought in whom nobody, not even King Philip himself, could master. This horse, Bucephalus by name, was destined to become one of the most famous horses in history.

Bucephalus was an enormous animal. This black giant, the scouts told Philip, had been extremely expensive; the price paid for him had been thirteen talents. It is very difficult to calculate what a talent would be worth in

American dollars, but it was considered to be an imposing sum. One talent was probably equal to $40,000, so that Bucephalus had cost the equivalent of $520,000, a lot of money for a horse.

Now as he watched the animal, Alexander noticed something peculiar, and his muscles became taut. Bucephalus, snorting with rage and acting like a wild beast (which indeed he was), refused to be mounted. He would shy violently each time he heard a voice. No one could get near him, much less swing up on his naked back.

King Philip, who had a hasty temper, saw that Bucephalus was indeed unmanageable. In disgust, he shouted an order to have the horse taken away and returned to the market.

Alexander leapt down from the fence. "No, no!" he cried. He rushed toward Philip and the horse, muttering excitedly to himself, "What a wonderful beast they are turning away! They don't know how to handle him!"

With youthful eloquence the boy appealed to his father not to send Bucephalus back to the market.

Philip looked at Alexander with cool appraisal, and

then at the wildly plunging horse. "Who could ride him?" Philip asked.

"I can," said Alexander.

Philip, who liked to treat his son like an adult, exclaimed, "And if you do not, what will you forfeit for your rashness?"

"I will pay the whole price of the horse," replied Alexander.

Thirteen talents, the price of Bucephalus, was much more money than Alexander had in the world. If he were to lose, he would have to mortgage his future to pay his father back.

"All right," said Philip. "Agreed."

The boy ran up to the giant horse, from whose eyes fury and terror were still darting. Grasping the bridle quickly, Alexander turned the animal full-face into the burning sun and kept him pointed in that direction.

The tough old courtiers around Philip were still laughing at the boy's bet. However, Philip, who tried to be a good father whenever he had time, had become alarmed lest his son be thrown and hurt. Now, as he watched the scene before him, the king's fears began to leave him and pride took their place.

Alexander was speaking gently to Bucephalus, clapping him on the back with a reassuring gesture. After a few minutes the horse's rapid panting began to slow down—a sign that he had become less agitated. He lowered his majestic head for a fraction of a second, and Alexander, with one bound, took advantage of this movement to leap up on the animal's back.

Alexander continued to keep Bucephalus pointed steadily toward the sun and soon this huge, ferocious beast walked as tamely as a faithful dog. Yet Alexander did not even strike him. He held the reins hard, eased his mount into a canter, and finally spurred him to a full gallop. The courtiers watched in amazement, hardly believing what their eyes reported.

Alexander then returned to where Philip stood openmouthed. When the boy dismounted, his father clutched him with pride and happiness.

To master Bucephalus was easy, Alexander explained. He had noticed that when the animal was first led out into the open courtyard his back was to the sun. Thus, his body cast a shadow that terrified him. The more he plunged and danced, the more frightening was the movement of the shadow. The boy shrewdly watched for his chance and turned the horse around, so that the shadow was not before him. Then he waited till Bucephalus tamed down.

Philip kissed Alexander on the head. "My son," he declared, with great emotion, "Macedonia will not be big enough for you. You will need a kingdom of your own!"

For years and years Alexander loved Bucephalus, and Bucephalus loved him in return. Almost always Bucephalus was the horse that he chose to ride in battle, and the gallant, flying figure of the blond young man on the huge black horse became a symbol of certain victory to the Macedonians. In time, Bucephalus became too old to fight, but Alexander always kept him with him. In fact, when Bucephalus was so aged that he could hardly walk, Alexander would nevertheless mount him before a battle and ride in sight of his troops for a few moments. This would encourage and stimulate them. Then he would change to another horse.

Bucephalus died sixteen years after that sunny spring morning in Pella when Alexander was the first human being ever to ride him. Alexander gave him a solemn funeral, and even named a city after him. The ruins of this city still exist today, in Kashmir, one of the far-off countries conquered by Alexander.

CHAPTER 2

IN THOSE DAYS GREECE WAS LIKE THIS . . .

IN THOSE DAYS THE EASTERN MEDITER-
ranean was the center of the universe. Athens, the chief
city of Greece, had a position, geographically and cultur-
ally, something like that of New York today.

But men did not know much of what lay beyond. The
Greeks knew their own seacoast well, their own rivers,
islands, valleys, and steep mountains. They had crossed
the Aegean Sea and built colonies along the coast of Asia
Minor, and they had penetrated westward into Sicily.
The Greek world was a kind of luminous circle, but
beyond its outer fringes all was darkness.

If a Greek looked north, he would know that Macedonia and Thrace existed, but beyond those countries there were only the barbarians—savage marauders who lived in the Danube area. Looking west and southwest, he would know about the great trading city of Carthage, on the African coast. Daring explorers had even reached the Straits of Gibraltar, which were called the Pillars of Hercules. But when Alexander was born, even Rome was little known outside Italy.

To the south, the Greeks had some knowledge of Egypt, and to the east, they had good reason to know a great deal about Persia and the huge and dangerous Persian Empire. Beyond that was India of which the Greeks had heard, although few of them had ever been there. Beyond India was China, a land unknown to the Greeks even by name.

Yet most of the world that was known at that time to the Greeks and Macedonians was eventually conquered by Alexander. This is what makes him so important to history. China he never reached, and he did not go westward (toward Italy) at all. But he conquered practically everything else.

This was an achievement so remarkable, so extraordinary, that it has challenged the minds of men ever since. Alexander was the first of those titans like Caesar and Napoleon who, partly by accident and partly by design, set out to gather the whole world into their fists, unify it, rule it, and enlighten it.

He sought to make the entire world his own, and almost succeeded. Hence, even though his career was short-lived, it is one of the most dazzling landmarks of all time.

Greece, then as now, looks like a many-fingered hand dangling down into the water. It is an arid little country, prickly with mountains and pockmarked with shallow hidden valleys. Its long, rough, jagged coastline is indented with many bays and inlets, and the surrounding waters are full of islands of surpassing beauty.

Originally, in about 4,000 B.C., the whole Greek area, including the islands, was populated by a people of whom we know little. The civilization they built, which we call "Aegean," reached its peak on the island of Crete. The findings of present-day archeologists have revealed how amazingly advanced these Cretans were in some ways, though in other ways they were half-savage. One picturesque detail is that they were the first people in history to have bathrooms and plumbing with running water.

In time, groups of marauders, called Hellenes, came down from the north and conquered and displaced the early Aegeans. Gradually, over long centuries, the Hellenes set up their own civilization, which spread over Greece and penetrated to the neighboring islands and into many coastal towns in Asia Minor. These Hellenes were an Aryan-speaking people (in other words, descendants of prehistoric people who spoke Indo-European), and their original home had been the savage area around the Danube River.

The early Greeks, as they developed, became what we would call today very strong individualists. They were great traders and voyagers, but they liked to stick close to their own small communities. Local pride and patriotism had great importance for them, and as their civilization advanced Greece became divided into a number of rival city-states, such as Athens, Thebes, and Sparta.

Greek geography was another factor that tended to split Greece into sections. It was not easy to clamber over the steep rocks, push down through the narrow twisting valleys, and get from one city to the next. Communications—the various means of connecting one community with another—were difficult and few.

Such handicaps could not hold back a people as clever as the Greeks. Right from the beginning, as soon as they emerged from barbarism, they showed signs of their great ambition, intelligence, and talent. They were good soldiers, alert seamen, and sharp traders with a fondness for bargaining. They lived simply, and the bases of their household economy were bread, olive oil, and wine.

No people in history ever gave so much to the human race, in so short a time, as the ancient Greeks. They produced architectural monuments as noble as the

Parthenon. They produced in rapid succession four of the greatest dramatists who ever lived—Sophocles, Euripides, Aeschylus, and Aristophanes. They produced one of the most brilliant statesmen who ever lived, Pericles, and two of the greatest historians, Thucydides and Herodotus. They produced scientists of the first rank, and three philosophers whose thought has done so much good for the world that their names are household words today—Socrates, Plato, and Aristotle.

Perhaps most important to us is the fact that the Greeks were the first people to evolve the political system that we call democracy. It was not quite the same kind of democracy as ours is today. But the Greeks had a firm belief in good citizenship. They despised politicians who cheated and swindled the common man; they believed deeply in civil rights and civil liberties and were prepared to fight for them.

Two tragedies, in time, struck the Greeks. Both were wars, and wars are always tragedies, even if you win them.

The Persians, over in continental Asia, decided to

attack and wipe out the Greeks, and made several attempts at invasion. Great battles took place around 490 B.C. at Marathon, Thermopylae, Salamis, and elsewhere. The Greeks, who were separated by local jealousies, finally got together and defeated the Persian invaders, but at a frightful cost.

Later came the Peloponnesian War, from 431 to 404 B.C. This war between Athens and Sparta was both damaging and unnecessary. The Greeks paid a severe penalty for being so blindly self-divided. The country came close to ruin as a result; it lay inert, exhausted, and an easy prey to the next conqueror.

Directly above Greece is Macedonia. Macedonia was— and is—a mixed-up place nationally, a confused tent of peoples. When we talk about something full of different and contrasting elements today, like a fruit salad, we call it a "Macedon."

The Macedonians, like the Greeks, were descendants of the wild barbarians in the unknown north. They were crude, fierce, bold, and high-spirited. They differed strongly from the more civilized Greeks in some ways; on the other hand they resembled them, too. They were like cousins. The Macedonians, a rough people, never produced any artists or dramatists or philosophers. But they produced King Philip—and Alexander.

CHAPTER 3

PHILIP, THE KING, AND OLYMPIAS, HIS QUEEN

THE LINE OF ALEXANDER'S LIFE IS BOLD AND sharp. From first to last, from birth to death, it is etched with dramatic clarity. He was born to conquer the world, and everything of importance that happened to him was a step toward the fulfillment of this ambition. But at the same time he had to struggle ceaselessly with his own self, his own wayward character.

To tell this story properly it is necessary to begin with Alexander's birth, heritage, and background. Not only did he have an extraordinary father, Philip, the hot-tempered king, but an extraordinary mother, too, whose name was Olympias. She was a ferocious woman.

Hot-tempered parents are apt to produce a hot-tempered child, and when Alexander reached manhood he often had great difficulty controlling his temper. In fact this bad temper, in the end, helped to kill him.

Nobody knows much about the origins of Philip's family. The few kings that are left today like to trace their ancestries as far back as possible, but we know little of Philip's family except that *his* father was a barbarian king named Amyntas II. We know, too, that Amyntas reached the throne of Macedonia after a series of family murders.

One fact that has come down from the old chroniclers is that Philip's mother was proud of herself because, when she was a very old lady, she learned to read and write. This shows how primitive the Macedonian court circle was. Philip was pleased by his mother's accomplishment, because he always put a great value on education. But comparatively few Macedonians—even in the leading families—knew how to read and write in those days. What they did know were such things as the best methods of making a battle-ax, or of skinning a goat.

Philip became King of Macedonia in 359 B.C., when he was twenty-three. He was an extremely enlightened king, one of the greatest kings in all history. He is also one of the few examples in history of a great father who was followed by a great son. Usually, for some mysterious reason, the sons of great fathers do not turn out particularly well. Maybe they try too hard to equal their fathers' reputations, instead of developing their own talents and abilities.

Although Philip and Alexander were alike in being great rulers, they differed in appearance. Philip had thick curly hair and a heavy dark beard. His nose was what we call "Greek"—straight with no kink between it and the forehead—but it had been broken several times, and so looked crooked. He was blind in one eye. Most of the time he wore armor, or else rough country clothes. He limped, from an old wound, and one of his arms was lame, also from a wound.

When Alexander grew up, he often showed sympathy for his father's wounds. Once Philip cried out in pain from his crippled leg, and the boy said, "Don't worry, Father. Every step you take, even if it is painful, reminds us of your victories!"

Philip, after he acceded to the Macedonian throne, had two great ambitions: first, to unify the Greeks, and second, to conquer the whole world. In some respects Philip resembled several modern dictators—he wanted to beat everybody and then hold them together. He did not understand what we call democracy.

Although he succeeded in the first ambition, he did not live long enough to achieve the second. That was to become the accomplishment of his son, Alexander.

Philip admired Greek culture and Greek brains. He ordered that Attic Greek, the kind of Greek spoken in Athens, become the language of his court instead of the crude Macedonian dialect. He had profound respect for a Greek philosopher, Isocrates, who preached that Greece must at all costs be unified.

On the other hand, Philip was often irritated by the Greeks because of their constant petty quarreling. He thought it was stupid and silly of them to have wasted their energies for twenty-seven years fighting the Peloponnesian War.

Of course, the fact that the Greeks were quarreling and fighting amongst themselves made it easier, when the time came, for this tough, unyielding Philip to conquer them.

When Philip was about twenty-five years old, he took a trip to the island of Samothrace where he met a young woman named Olympias. She was an orphan, of royal blood, for her father had been the King of Epirus. This was a small, undeveloped country which lay directly to the west of Macedonia and which, like Macedonia, was strongly under Greek influence.

Olympias had pitch-black hair, burning eyes, and a complicated personality. She was a good match, for she was the heiress to the neighboring kingdom, and Philip fell in love with her.

He had gone to Samothrace to attend a religious festival which was celebrated with pagan rites, and he discovered that Olympias was fascinated by these barbarous ceremonies. She had a wild, reckless love for oracles, prophecies, omens, and witches.

Nevertheless Philip asked her to marry him, and she quickly accepted. They returned together to Macedonia, and Olympias became Philip's queen. In 356 B.C., Alexander, whom we call the Great, was born.

Most remarkable men, it seems, have remarkable mothers, probably because the mother puts so much of her self into the boy as he grows up. Olympias was certainly remarkable. Today, we would call her a vicious shrew.

Philip began to be angry with her when she insisted on keeping snakes in their room at night. No husband likes snakes to be crawling around the bed. But Olympias said that they were tame, and would not do Philip any harm. Besides, she insisted, they were holy.

This same strange wildness seemed to enter into

everything that Olympias did. It even touched her affection for her son, for she loved Alexander to distraction, and was madly jealous and possessive. This love was the cause of many of the wicked and terrible things she did in her long lifetime.

By another, previous wife, Philip had had a son named Arrhidaeus, who was thus Alexander's half-brother. Arrhidaeus grew up to be half-witted, and some historians say that Olympias actually poisoned this helpless boy with a magical herb, so that he would always be mentally subnormal. Her motive was to make it impossible for him ever to become a rival to Alexander.

Be this as it may, Alexander had a great love for Olympias all his life. She irritated him sometimes— mostly when, as mothers will, she did not take him seriously enough. During his campaigns in Asia, as he was conquering the world, he never failed to write her dutiful letters once a month or so.

On the night that Olympias gave birth to Alexander, Philip was down in Greece, fighting. A trusted courier brought him the news, along with two other messages. One of these reported that the Macedonians had just won an important battle in Illyria; the other said that one of Philip's horses had just won first prize in the Olympic Games. So the King had three bits of good news all at once. This would bring luck, he thought.

CHAPTER 4

ALEXANDER GROWS UP

ALEXANDER LEARNED EARLY IN HIS YOUTH that he was Crown Prince, and that some day he would inherit the Macedonian throne. He had the kind of special upbringing that crown princes are apt to get—he was pampered in some ways, and severely disciplined in others.

From the very beginning, he appears to have had a violently ambitious streak. When he was about twelve a courier brought him the news that Philip had won a great battle. Alexander wailed, "If my father wins any more battles, there won't be anything left for *me* to conquer!"

Although Alexander was good at sports, he was often

bored by them. He disliked fisticuffs and wrestling, which were the major sports for boys at that time. He was fond of hunting. He had quick reflexes, and was fleet of foot. One of the courtiers, noticing how well Alexander ran, suggested that he should compete in the next Olympic foot-races.

He replied loftily, with words that showed he was somewhat spoiled, "I won't run against anybody except kings!"

Then, at about this time, came the encounter with Bucephalus, which has already been described. Alexander's budding character began to show some other attributes for which he became famous—courage, cleverness, and complete self-confidence.

Philip wanted Alexander to have as good an education as the world could provide. To this end, the King persuaded Aristotle, the venerable Athenian philosopher and scientist, to come up to Pella to be the boy's tutor. This is as if Albert Einstein were to become the tutor of some boy of royal blood.

Philip paid Aristotle a very large sum to teach

Alexander, and the experiment was a great success. Aristotle's principal claim to fame, at that time, was that he had arranged in an orderly way the world's existing store of knowledge in such fields as medicine, politics, law, and natural history.

Aristotle introduced young Alexander to each of these and other subjects, taught him the delights of using his reasoning powers, and in particular opened up to him the world of great books.

The book Alexander liked best was Homer's *Iliad,* and under Aristotle's guidance he learned almost the whole of this by heart. Alexander's mind and imagination were permanently fired by the *Iliad,* with its wonderful old stories of the Greek heroes in the Trojan War. For years thereafter, in all his campaigns, he always kept two things under his pillow at night—a dagger for protection, and the *Iliad.*

Philip was delighted by the way Aristotle and the young prince got along together. It happened that, in one of his wars, Philip had taken and destroyed the town where Aristotle was born. So now, to do penance for this act and as a gesture of thanks to the great philosopher, he ordered the whole town rebuilt and permitted its exiled citizens to return.

Alexander said years later, "It was my father who gave me life. But it was Aristotle who taught me how to live."

In addition to his other gifts, Alexander began to show strong artistic tendencies. He liked music and learned to play the harp. This alarmed Philip, who began to fear that if the Crown Prince became too absorbed in the arts, he would lose interest in war and conquest. As a corrective, he made Alexander do a lot of tough campaigning with the troops.

It is curious that most kings throughout history have seemingly cared little about what might happen after their deaths, and have tended to neglect the education of their sons. Philip was different. Deliberately, and with great seriousness, he trained Alexander to be a king. Step by step, he sought to prepare the boy for the enormous responsibilities that would be his as king of the rapidly growing Macedonian empire.

There are some historians today who think that

Alexander might never have amounted to much if it had not been for Philip's training and example. Philip really *made* Alexander. It was Philip who did the spade work; Alexander followed with the plow. Philip marked out the path—the path to warfare against the Persians and world conquest; Alexander did little but develop it.

When the boy was about seventeen, Philip decided that it was time for Alexander to have his baptism of fire, so he was in temporary charge of affairs in Pella while his father went to Greece.

As soon as Philip's back was turned, a wild tribe in the north, thinking to take advantage of Alexander's youth and inexperience, started a revolt. Promptly Alexander acted. He marched against the rebels, beat them in battle, and captured their chief city.

Philip was vastly pleased. Then Alexander, who was already beginning to show signs of too much vanity, renamed the beaten city after himself—Alexandropolis!— as he was to do with many other cities later.

During this period, Philip was fighting constantly. In Greece, there were two parties—pro-Philip and anti-

Philip. The leader of those who wanted to resist Philip's effort to force Greece into unity was the celebrated orator Demosthenes. The speeches he made attacking Philip have been called "Philippics" ever since.

The climax to Philip's conquest of Greece was the battle of Chaeronea, fought in 338 B.C. Philip was at the full height of his powers; Alexander, at eighteen, had reached the threshold of young manhood. To test his son further, Philip gave him command of the cavalry. Alexander met the test, and fought like a madman, charging the Thebans at the head of his men. This charge decided the battle.

Philip wanted to make friends with the Greeks after Chaeronea. He was very shrewd. Instead of making a vengeful peace, he sent Alexander to Athens as a good-will emissary. The young prince brought to the city the ashes of the Athenians who had died honorably in the battle. With him went his closest friend, Hephaestion— a man destined to play an important role in Alexander's life.

Alexander was asked to say something to the people of

Athens when he arrived. He replied modestly, "My father and Chaeronea speak, not I."

Demosthenes fled after this, and Philip was appointed Captain-General of all Greece (except Sparta) for the coming struggle against the Persians.

Meantime, things were not going well at home. By this time Philip was sick and tired of Olympias. She bored him and he hated her sorcerers, soothsayers, and snakes. So, as kings were allowed to do in those days, he took a second wife, who was a native Macedonian and whose name was Cleopatra. (She is not to be confused with Cleopatra, the beautiful Queen of Egypt who lived three centuries later.)

Upon Philip's second marriage, Olympias went wild with rage. Her jealousy of Cleopatra was boundless, and she determined to get rid of her rival by fair means or foul.

Her first step was subtle. To achieve her end, Olympias worked indirectly through Alexander. Using him as a tool, she slowly poisoned his mind against his father.

Her work bore fruit at the sumptuous feast which

Philip gave to celebrate his marriage to Cleopatra. One of Cleopatra's uncles got very drunk. He made a speech, pointing out that, whereas Olympias came from Epirus, Cleopatra was a native Macedonian. Then he toasted Philip and Cleopatra, expressing the hope that they would soon have a son, who would be a pure Macedonian and hence a good successor to the throne.

Alexander rose, hot with fury. "What about me, you traitor!" he shouted at the drunken uncle. "Am I not the lawful heir?"

Philip was very drunk, too. He staggered to his feet, and drew his sword, fumbling at it. But whether he was going to attack Alexander or Cleopatra's insolent uncle we do not know, because he slipped heavily—he was lame—and crashed noisily to the floor.

Alexander walked up to him as he lay there, helpless. His youthful voice quivered with contempt. "Look, Macedonians!" he cried. "This man, my father, says he is going to lead you from country to country in Asia! But he can't even stand up and walk from one table to the next!"

CHAPTER 5

ALEXANDER BECOMES KING

A TERRIBLE CRISIS FOLLOWED THIS AWFUL scene. Alexander had publicly insulted the King, his father, and the whole court wondered what would happen when Philip, with his fierce temper, sobered up. What revenge would Philip take? How would he punish Alexander?

Actually he behaved quite moderately. Probably his marriage to Cleopatra had given him a guilty conscience, and, more than likely, he was sorry for having been so drunk. At any rate, the historians differ in their versions of what followed.

One story is that Philip, maintaining his royal dignity, promptly exiled Olympias to her native Epirus and that Alexander dutifully went with his mother.

The other is that Alexander took the initiative, insisting that Olympias leave Philip at once, and that he himself took her back to Epirus, and stayed with her there.

But Alexander's eyes always followed the beckoning gleam of power. He always wanted to be where big things were happening. After a time Philip sounded him out— would he come back? Philip's motive did not spring merely from parental affection. He wanted Alexander close to him, close to the throne, close to Pella, as a sign of unity.

After a time Alexander accepted Philip's offer of reconciliation, and returned to the court.

When he went back Philip attempted to resume their old relationship, but Alexander, strongly under the influence of Olympias, had grown to hate his father. Philip tried in every possible way to regain the boy's respect and affection, but Alexander stayed cold, suspicious, and aloof. Father and son never became close again.

Alexander was now nineteen. Another episode added to his unfriendly feeling toward Philip. A prince in Caria, out in Asia Minor, sent an emissary to Macedonia. He wanted to offer his daughter in marriage to Philip's other son, Arrhidaeus, Alexander's half-brother, the boy whose mind had not fully developed.

When Olympias heard of this marriage offer, she wrote to Alexander to arouse his suspicions of his father. She said that if Philip approved of this offer, by which Arrhidaeus would become the husband of a princess, it could only mean that the King was secretly planning to disinherit Alexander. In time Arrhidaeus, the half-imbecile, would succeed to the throne!

Probably Philip had no such idea at all. But Alexander, spurred on by Olympias, determined to outwit him. He sent a messenger of his own out to Caria, to say that he, Alexander, would be glad to marry the Carian princess instead of Arrhidaeus.

Philip got wind of this development, and was furious. But, more than furious, he was sad. It hurt him very much that Alexander should be so stupid and base as to think that he, Philip, had ever had any idea of depriving him of his rightful throne.

Philip still wanted desperately, with all the pride of a father, to win Alexander back. But he did not know quite how to handle his son. What happened finally was that Philip lost his temper. He told Alexander frankly that he was not worthy of becoming a king if, out of spite, he threw himself away by marriage to a barbarian princess in Asia.

Alexander, who wanted to be absolutely sure of the throne, at last gave up the idea of marrying the girl in far-off Caria. But because Alexander had even thought of such a marriage, Philip punished him by sending into exile half a dozen of his best friends. Meantime, Philip had a son by Cleopatra.

The uncle of Cleopatra had mistreated Pausanias, a man in Philip's court. When he complained to Philip, Pausanias got no satisfaction whatever. Enraged he turned to Olympias and her friends. A few days later Philip was assassinated; the murderer was Pausanias.

Practically at the same moment that he killed Philip,

Pausanias himself was slain by loyal members of Philip's bodyguard.

People at once accused Olympias of having a hand in the plot to murder the King, but this seemed to bother her very little. Her revenge was complete. Philip was dead, and Alexander became king. Then, as if to make things doubly sure, Olympias had both Cleopatra and her infant son murdered, too!

Such was the dark, bloody backdrop to Alexander's accession to the throne. There were even whispers that he, Alexander, was a member of the conspiracy to murder Philip, but such stories have never been proved.

So, in 336 B.C., at the age of twenty, Alexander became King of Macedon. Nobody had the faintest idea that he was destined to be king not merely of Macedonia and Greece but of almost the whole known world.

PART TWO

CHAPTER 6

THE BEGINNING OF THE REIGN

ALTHOUGH HE WAS ONLY TWENTY, ALEXANDER'S character was by this time almost completely formed. Like most creative people, he was full of contrasts. He was affectionate, generous, and loyal. Plutarch, the old chronicler who gives us the best picture of him available, makes a strong point of how gentle he usually was. He never spared himself, he liked to do services for others, and he loved his friends.

But—this is the other side—he had no control of his temper and, in later life, often went into crazy fits of debauchery. Worst of all, he showed great cruelty on many occasions.

He had one important quality that almost all great men have—he was swift. He made decisions quickly, and moved with a snap. His reflexes were those of a prize fighter, darting in for the kill.

Alexander was tremendously vain. And why not? He knew his own quality. He liked to name cities for himself. He liked to have his portrait painted, showing his handsome profile. He continually had coins and medals made, and it is from these, scattered all over the antique world, and discovered by accident or dug up in later centuries, that we know how he looked.

In those days it was extremely rare for men to be clean-shaven, but Alexander never wore a beard. By shaving he set a fashion that has lasted more that two thousand years.

In the early years of his reign, he took good care of his health. He exercised regularly, and ate and drank in moderation. Once he told a friend, "A night march is my breakfast, and a light breakfast is my dinner." He paid almost no attention to girls. He liked plenty of sleep and sometimes slept all day, even when there was a lot of business waiting to be done.

He cared nothing for wealth or pleasure, Plutarch tells us, but only for war and honor.

He picked men shrewdly, and they loved him. Two of his closest friends, at least, are profoundly important in his story—Cleitus and Hephaestion. They were completely different types of men. Cleitus, a tough battalion commander, known by the nickname of "Black" Cleitus, was a fighter pure and simple. Hephaestion was much more sensitive and delicate, and served for years as Alexander's aide-de-camp. Both met death in Alexander's service, as we shall see.

Alexander's best general was named Parmenio, an older man who had served Philip. Parmenio, too, met a cruel death. Parmenio's son, Philotas, was another of Alexander's intimate, trusted friends.

The story would not be complete without mention of the fine old soldier, Antipater, whom Alexander never saw after he left Greece. It was Antipater who stayed behind, ran the government, and kept Macedonia and Greece in order for year after year.

Alexander's character may seem puzzling in some respects, but in the light of what we know today he is not too difficult to understand. Like many brilliant men, he was unstable—which means that he ran from one extreme to another, and tried to live two lives at once. On one hand, he was a dreamer. On the other, he was a man of action. The two sides to his nature were always at war within him, for each one tried to get the upper hand. It was because of this internal conflict that Alexander was destroyed in the end.

Alexander had plenty to do from the moment he ascended the throne. Fortunately, no one had questioned his right to take his father's place. The country, the government, and Philip's superlatively well-trained army all fell into his lap. Yet Alexander, a jealous person, was slow to acknowledge what his father had done for him. "All I got from my father was debts," he complained bitterly. And it was true that the treasury was almost empty.

Philip had been fighting to unify Greece into submission for a long time, and wars cost money.

Alexander did, however, immediately make at least one gesture of respect to his great father's memory. He rounded up and punished all the conspirators in the murder plot, and rebuked his mother severely for having murdered Cleopatra.

As soon as the rebellious, independent-minded Greeks heard that Philip was dead, they began to get restless. They knew little about Alexander, but they should have remembered how well he had fought at Chaeronea. To them he was just a youngster, completely green. They could not have been more wrong.

At this time Greece seemed to be coming apart at the seams. Even Macedonia was shaken to some extent, by the shock of Philip's untimely death. Everybody thought that Alexander would at once go down to Greece and try to pacify it. But, though the throne was hardly warm under him, he fooled everybody and moved in exactly the opposite direction.

By training and instinct Alexander sensed a profound

military truth, as valid today as it was then, that a good commander must always protect the lines of supply and communication that are behind him. Otherwise it is not safe to advance.

So, in 335 B.C., after restoring order in Macedonia and getting from the Greek states a promise to behave (in return for which he gave them local freedom), Alexander leapt up to the north. The march he made was, by any standards, little short of miraculous. The northern country was completely savage and unmapped—a roadless wilderness. But in an incredibly short time Alexander led his troops to the far-off Danube, established headquarters in what is now Bucharest, the capital of Romania, and soundly beat the tribesmen who had threatened to rise against him.

From that time until his death, Alexander never had trouble with the northern barbarians. His frontier remained secure.

Then, triumphant, he returned and set about dealing with Greece. Bitterly he remembered Demosthenes, the orator who had thundered against Philip. He proclaimed, "Demosthenes will find out that I was a child when I conquered the barbarians in Thrace last week, that I became a youth yesterday when I crossed into Greece from the plains of Thessaly, and that now, outside the walls of Athens, I am a man!"

Alexander's basic ambition was to defeat the Persians, and the Greeks knew it well. Some Greeks approved of this prospect, and hence took Alexander's side. But others opposed him with great vigor, because it was their belief that an expedition against Persia would be foolhardy and expensive. They wanted to get along with the Persians, even if this meant submitting to them. After all, the Greeks' trade with Persia made a lot of money!

A serious revolt against the Macedonians broke out in Thebes, a sacred city of Greece. Alexander offered to forgive the Thebans if they would surrender. They scorned his peace terms unless Alexander would also turn over to them two of his closest associates, Antipater and Philotas, whom they hated and wanted to kill. Alexander refused.

So he marched against Thebes, took it, and burned the

city to the ground. Thirty thousand Thebans were sold into slavery, and six thousand Thebans were killed. Those were gigantic casualty lists for those days. In the entire city of Thebes, Alexander spared exactly one house—the home of the celebrated poet, Pindar. He had always liked Pindar's poetry.

This is the first of a long series of atrocities charged against Alexander. It was wicked of him to have had so many people killed and to have sacked and burned such a fine city as Thebes. But in this period of history it was customary to punish cities that revolted. Alexander felt that he had to make an example of Thebes, in order to teach the other Greeks a lesson.

It did teach them a lesson, too. From that time until the end of his far-flung campaigns, Alexander never had any trouble holding the Greeks in line.

Another thing is certain. He must have felt, even if the destruction of Thebes was necessary, that he had done a serious wrong, because he had a guilty conscience about Thebes ever after. As if to make amends, in later years, he always tried to do favors for any Thebans he chanced to meet.

Alexander's character did not change after Thebes. Repeatedly he did things that he knew were wrong, but he did them anyway, and was always sorry later. Yet he occasionally proved that he was capable of mercy.

This was shown in something that happened immediately after the battle of Thebes, when Alexander's men brought to him a Theban woman who had been taken prisoner. It appeared that she had defended her house staunchly when the Macedonians came with fire and sword, and they had cruelly attacked her. One Macedonian trooper asked if she had any gold, and she answered yes—it was hidden deep in a well in the back yard. Then, when he peered down the well, she pushed him in and killed him by tossing heavy stones on him. Now this lady was being brought to Alexander for judgment. When she finished telling her story, Alexander at once gave orders that she should be freed, because he felt that she was a gallant woman even though she had killed one of his captains.

One of the great personalities in Greece at this time was Diogenes. He was what today we would call an eccentric. He lived in a barrel and did nothing except seek the truth.

Alexander was curious about Diogenes and went to see him. Diogenes, who was very old, was sitting out in the warm sun, half-naked, and although he had no worldly goods, he was happy. Alexander asked if he could do anything for him.

"Yes," replied Diogenes. "Move out of the sun. Your shadow is in my way."

Alexander's men were shocked by such boldness. But Alexander, smiling, said to them, "Laugh if you want, but if I were not Alexander, the man I would like to be is Diogenes."

Alexander decided to visit Delphi, the seat of a celebrated oracle. Whatever this oracle told a person, whether good news or bad, always turned out to be true—or so people thought. The oracle was considered to be absolutely fool-proof.

But Alexander got a considerable shock—the Delphi

priestess refused to tell him anything. She said that because the holy signs were not good that day, she would prefer not to make any prophecies. Angered, Alexander hauled her into the temple to make her do her job. This action must have impressed the priestess mightily, because she then pronounced an omen very favorable. "Young man," she declared, "you are going to be invincible."

Another thing happened that impressed the superstitious, which, at that time, meant everybody. A statue of the hero Orpheus, made out of cypress wood, began to sweat. Some of Alexander's friends thought that this was a bad sign, and were frightened. However, a soothsayer calmed them by explaining that this meant merely that Alexander was going to have such a great career that poets, until the end of time, would sweat out songs about him. And, indeed, this is what has happened.

CHAPTER 7

PERSIA,
A DISTANT COUNTRY

NOW, BEFORE PROCEEDING TO TELL THE STORY of Alexander's attack on Asia, let us say a word or two about the Persians, his first enemies there.

Persia still exists as a country, but nowadays it is called Iran. Of course it is nowhere near as big as it was during Alexander's boyhood, when it was an enormous empire, covering half the known world.

Today Persia is important and interesting chiefly because it has gigantic reserves of oil. The oil lay under the red, clayey earth then as now, but Alexander had no idea that it existed—or, rather, that it was valuable.

Just in passing, we might mention that Plutarch tells a little story about how some of Alexander's men, digging around on Persian soil, found a strange liquid which burned fiercely. It was like nothing they had ever seen before. One man doused himself with it and then set fire to his clothes—he wanted to prove that this peculiar, unknown liquid *did* burn. It certainly did, and he was almost burned to death. So oil, or petroleum, was discovered. Then centuries passed before man learned to find this precious stuff in quantity, and make use of it.

The Persians, like the Greeks, came originally out of the wild hills, forests, and steppes in the north. Like the Greeks, they were an Aryan-speaking people who were at first nomads, then herdsmen, then ferocious raiders.

Whereas the Greeks had descended from the Danube area of what is now Europe, the Persians came from places farther east, in the borderline region between Europe and Asia. Even so, Greeks and Persians resembled one another to a certain degree.

Constant travels and migrations mixed up the various peoples. During prolonged movements of tribes and conquests, the men and women of different races and nations married and inter-married. Asia near the Caspian and Black Sea was a territory from which peoples spread out like sand swept by the wind. Invading hordes rolled out from the Russian steppes and mingled with other tribes.

Like the Greeks, the Persians displaced the original inhabitants in various places, as they penetrated south. In time they planted themselves in the region that, along with Egypt, was the first great site of civilization—the fertile valley made by the Tigris and Euphrates rivers in Mesopotamia, or, as we say today, Iraq.

All sorts of kingdoms, or empires, had already existed in this marvelously fertile region—Sumerian, Babylonian, Assyrian and Chaldean. There had been famous law-givers, like Hammurabi, and notoriously cruel kings, like Nebuchadnezzar.

Important cities grew and flourished here, as well as in the arid Persian plateau. There was Babylon, on the Euphrates, which is nothing but a ruin now, a haunt for archeologists. Nineveh, on the Tigris, is the site of the modern oil town, Mosul. Ecbatana, in northern Persia, is called Hamadan today. Susa, another capital, was in southern Persia.

The first great Persian king, Cyrus the Great, came to the throne in 550 B.C., about two hundred years before Alexander. He consolidated the Persian empire, trying to make one nation of such different people as the Medes, the Lydians, the Armenians, and so on. His kingdom stretched all the way from the Greek colonies in Asia Minor to the gates of India.

Another Persian king of consequence was Darius I who extended his rule to parts of Europe. Darius held so much territory that his empire might be compared to Philip's as an elephant might be compared to a mouse. Nevertheless, the Greeks beat Darius and his Persians at Marathon.

Then, after Darius, came his son Xerxes, who continued the Persian wars against Greece, which we have mentioned in a preceding chapter. Xerxes was murdered in 465 B.C.

A period of decay followed, and the Persians never

attempted to attack Greece again. The king who reigned over Persia when Alexander set out was Darius III. He was nowhere near so strong as Cyrus, Darius I, or Xerxes. The Greeks always called the Persians "barbarians," but this term is not quite correct. Perhaps the Persians were not as civilized as the Athenian Greeks, but they were far from being savages. Persia was prosperous and well-ordered, and commerce flourished. The roads were good—much better than European roads of the time— and made a network holding the vast empire together. The Persians loved art, and their rugs and tiles are still among the most beautiful objects of art in the world.

If it is remembered that Persians and Greeks were closely related, it will be seen that Alexander's war against Persia was similar to a civil war—the most evil kind of war known to mankind. But people did not have such thoughts in those days.

CHAPTER 8

THE GREAT ADVENTURE BEGINS

SO ALEXANDER'S GREAT ADVENTURE BEGAN, the adventure which made his name imperishable— the conquest of Persia that became the conquest of the world. He set out in 334 B.C., about two years after he became King of Macedon. No such expedition had ever been known before, and few like it have ever occurred since.

First Alexander had to cross the Hellespont. Ahead of his army he sent Parmenio, who had been Philip's best general, to scout out the way. The Hellespont, known as the Dardanelles today, is the narrow strait of water that separates Europe from Asia.

The crossing proved unexpectedly easy, after a stiff march through Thrace (what is now northeastern Greece). The Persians, careless, let Alexander cross without resistance. He stood on the shores of Asia at last, in the land that is now Turkey.

He could not get thoughts of the Trojan War out of his head. He had a cushion of time, and so he relaxed a little, and then made a quick trip south along the beautiful, rocky Asia Minor coast, toward the site of Troy.

All that the *Iliad* told heroically—and still tells—was well known to Alexander. A thousand years or so before there had been a Greek military expedition to this same spot! Here the legendary Greek heroes had fought against the Trojans for ten mortal years, until they won by the trick of the Trojan Horse. Those heroes were very close and real to Alexander—Ulysses the wise, Nestor the ancient, Agamemnon, brave Ajax (who was stupid, too), Patroclus, Diomed, and the greatest of them all, Achilles.

When Alexander reached Troy, he sacrificed to the goddess Athena first. Then he found the grave of Achilles, made a speech over it, anointed it with oil (an old Greek custom), decorated it with flowers (the way we would do today), and finally danced around it naked (another old Greek custom).

One of his companions asked him if he would like to play on a harp, the harp that Paris had used. Paris was the Trojan hero who had caused the war by running away with the wife of the Greek King, Menelaus.

"No," replied Alexander. "Find me a Greek harp—the harp of Achilles. That is the only harp I will play."

Alexander soon returned to his base near the Hellespont, for there was serious business to attend to. The treasury was almost empty; he had only seventy talents left, and not more than a thirty-day supply of food for his army. But he wanted to give presents to his companions who were going to follow him. Making a swift decision, he distributed among them his royal property in Macedonia.

"My Lord," gasped Perdiccas, one of his best captains, "what are you keeping for yourself?"

Alexander answered with the single word, "Hope!"

Alexander started out with approximately 30,000 foot soldiers and 4,000 cavalry. This was not much, considering the scope of his plans. He left behind 12,000 men, under the redoubtable Antipater, to keep peace in Macedonia and Greece.

Against him, the Persians—with their enormous, sprawling empire of many races—could muster millions.

But Alexander had one important military advantage. From Philip he inherited something that really did win battles, something that has been famous in military history ever since—the Macedonian phalanx, or massed array of troops.

As built up by Philip, the Macedonian army consisted of several parts. First came between 1,200 and 2,000 mounted noblemen, lords of the realm, who were called the "King's Companions." Philip had drilled these officers and their men to maneuver and charge not as individuals but as a *unit,* something that may seem obvious to us now, but which had hitherto been unknown.

Second came the archers, who hovered on the flanks.

Third and most important came the celebrated phalanx, made up of infantry with long spears.

This phalanx moved as a unit, too, because Philip had contrived the idea of locking its members together, so to speak. They fought shield-to-shield, in rows, with their spears sticking out from what seemed to the enemy to be a solid wall of shields, and had a terrifying effect.

At the critical moment in every battle, while the cavalry was swooping along the flanks and the archers were sending their arrows overhead into the enemy mass, this phalanx would plunge forward to where it was needed most, with irresistible power. It was like a multihuman tank.

Artillery was another of Philip's inventions. He used machines that threw stones. Later Alexander improved on these catapults and learned how to use them to great tactical effect.

Alexander understood with wonderful insight the modern military principles of organization, mobility, quick charges, and, above all, the proper concentration of force. One of his maxims was "march divided, fight united." He had a superb knack for massing his best strength against the enemy's weakest point, at exactly the right moment.

Why did Alexander start out on his grandiose march so soon after reaching the throne? For one thing, he was an impatient young man by nature; for another, Philip had trained him from boyhood to think of nothing else.

What was his essential, basic motive? Did he want to beat Persia in a war of vengeance and then stop? Or did he have the idea, even in those first days, of conquering the rest of Asia, too? Probably it was a mixture of both. When he beat Persia, he just kept right on going.

Why did Alexander never return to Greece, even for a short visit? We do not know. Mainly he was too busy, and always thought that he would get back *some* day, without worrying when it would be. But it is strange that he had so little interest in his own country.

In any case, his campaigns proceeded without interruption until his death eleven years later, and he never saw his native land again.

CHAPTER 9

ALEXANDER WINS
HIS FIRST GREAT BATTLE

ALEXANDER'S SMALL, COMPACT, EFFICIENT army began to move forward. The Persians woke up—too late—and massed their forces at the first natural barrier, which was the River Granicus. But they did not yet take Alexander altogether seriously. We know now that their intelligence service was not very good.

Darius III, the king of Persia, who was known throughout Asia as the King of Kings, did not even bother to go to the battle personally. This was a mistake. But the Persians still thought that Alexander was a mere boy.

They were as indifferent to him as a mastadon might be to a bothersome fly.

The River Granicus is quite near the Hellespont, where Alexander had started his march into Asia. So he had not come very far, and his men were fresh.

He paused on the west bank of the Granicus, and looked at the Persian hosts on the other side. Where he stood the bank sloped gently. But the east bank, held by the Persians, was rocky and very steep. The time was the middle of the afternoon, about three o'clock.

Alexander held a quick council of war, after sending scouts to dip into the river and find out how swift and deep it was.

One of his commanders then mentioned that this was a bad time to fight, for it was a day in June. And, according to Macedonian tradition, June was an unlucky month for battle. Philip had always been careful not to fight in June.

Alexander said calmly, "Turn the calendar back. We will pretend that it is still May."

When the scouts returned, Parmenio said, "We should wait till tomorrow. The crossing is dangerous, and we do not know if there are any fords. Observe the sun, my Lord. It is too late today."

Alexander replied, "We crossed an arm of the open sea, at the Hellespont. The Hellespont will blush with shame if we are afraid to cross a mere river."

He mounted his horse forthwith, and the attack began. Alexander was the first man to plunge into the swirling water. The air became filled with Persian arrows as Bucephalus struggled with the current. At last Alexander managed to reach the steep east bank, unharmed but wet. The Persian bank was slippery with mud, but he scrambled up the incline, with his men following close behind.

The Persians charged with reckless ferocity, uttering great cries and whipping out their swords for hand-to-hand fighting. The struggle was fierce as more and more mounted Macedonians crossed the river.

Alexander, out in front, was a conspicuous target because of special marks on his shield and because he wore a helmet from which floated a long white plume. The Persians quickly realized that he was the king and went after him. First he was struck in the thigh by a dart. Then a Persian captain, slipping up from behind, hurled a lance at him. As it struck Alexander's shield, the impact was so great that the lance broke. The Persian captain then hauled out his battle-ax, and stretching himself up full-length on his stirrups, crashed the battle-ax down on Alexander's head. The blow was so tremendous that it cut off the crest of Alexander's helmet and carved his white plume apart. Bucephalus plunged and staggered, and Alexander fell. He would certainly have been killed then and there, but "Black" Cleitus rushed up in the nick of time and killed the Persian by running him straight through with his spear. Gasping, Alexander rose. Cleitus had saved his life.

By this time the Macedonian infantrymen had succeeded in swimming across the river, even though they were encumbered by armor. At the sight of the great numbers of enemy troops, the Persians began to break up and flee.

The chroniclers say that Persia lost around 20,000

infantrymen and 2,500 horsemen at this battle, whereas the total Macedonian casualties were exactly thirty-four. Of course this must be an exaggeration. But the Battle of the Granicus was over, and Alexander had won his first great victory in Asia.

CHAPTER 10

ALEXANDER CUTS THE GORDIAN KNOT, WINS A SECOND BATTLE, AND SACKS TYRE

ALEXANDER WAS NATURALLY DELIGHTED WITH himself after Granicus, and he made a big decision. Although it surprised people, it was nevertheless wise. Instead of chasing Darius and knocking him out, as was expected, he turned his back on the Persians and slowly went down the coast of Asia Minor, consolidating his position there and making sure of his communications back to Greece.

Alexander was an impetuous young man. It is a tribute

to his shrewdness as a military commander that on this occasion he took a somewhat conservative course, instead of starting out on a wild pursuit of Darius.

Systematically he proceeded to clean up Asia Minor. He took the cities of Halicarnassus and Miletus, and conquered the Pisidians, Phrygians, Paphlagonians, and Cappadocians. Actually this was not such hard work. News of the Battle of the Granicus spread fast, and nobody was particularly eager to tangle in combat with this victorious young man.

In Lycia, Alexander received an omen that pleased him mightily. A spring, swelling over its banks, threw out a copper plate. On it was engraved the message, "The kingdom of Persia will be destroyed by Greece." This increased Alexander's confidence in his own destiny, his own good luck.

A similar incident added to Alexander's belief that great things lay before him. On one occasion, he marched his army through the town of Gordium, which is near Ankara, the present capital of Turkey. It was said that

Gordium had once been ruled by a famous mythological king named Midas. He had been so wealthy that his name is still a synonym for vast riches.

Carefully guarded in a sacred building, since the days of Midas, was an old chariot. Its shaft was fastened to the axle by a knot of enormous complexity, called the Gordian Knot. This knot was celebrated all over the world because nobody had ever been able to untie it. And there was a legend that if any man should succeed in the impossible job of getting it loose, he would become King of Asia.

Alexander took one look at the huge knot, took out his sword, and with a single stroke sliced it apart.

Nobody else had ever thought of doing that. All those who had attempted to loosen the knot had tried to untie it with their fingers. Alexander smiled.

One day, when he was still hot from exercise, Alexander took a swim in an icy river. For the first time in his life, he became seriously ill. He had been trying to do so much that he had worn himself out. (This is never a good thing for a young—or old—man to do; nature is apt to take revenge on those who abuse her gifts.)

He had a prolonged fever and almost died. None of the ordinary doctors seemed to be able to help. Then, so weak that he could hardly sit up, Alexander called in a new physician named Philip the Acarnanian. But as the physician was about to begin the treatment, Alexander received an urgent message from Parmenio, who was away at the base camp. In the message Parmenio said he had just discovered that Philip the Acarnanian was actually an assassin, hired by King Darius to poison Alexander.

Alexander put Parmenio's letter under his pillow without saying anything. Philip then gave him a glass of medicine to swallow. As Alexander took the glass, he handed Philip the letter and then, deliberately, gulped down the medicine.

While Philip read Parmenio's warning, Alexander looked steadily at him. At last Philip finished reading, and he stared in amazement at the King. The charge that he was an assassin was false, but even so it was incredible that any man, even Alexander, could have been bold enough and sure enough of his own instincts to take such a chance.

After drinking the medicine, Alexander became much worse. He fainted, his speech failed him, and his legs turned cold. Then, slowly, he started to recover.

The major problem facing Alexander was still Darius. He would have to deal with the King of Kings sooner or later. After Granicus, Darius had realized that Alexander was an extremely dangerous opponent, and to resist him the Persian ruler had organized an army somewhat larger than Alexander's.

For a time the two kings played hide and seek all over the arid, desolate region between Turkey and Syria. Then Alexander, diving down into Cilicia, thought that at last he had trapped Darius. But at exactly this moment the Persian king, at the head of his forces, marched in the opposite direction to meet and vanquish *him*.

Thus, the two armies passed each other at night in parallel mountain passes. As a result, when they finally met, Alexander discovered that Darius was behind him, cutting off his own path to the sea. This was a difficult situation, but Alexander seemingly did not care and made the best of it. He loved to fight, no matter where, even if he appeared to be at a disadvantage.

The battle that followed is known to history as the battle of Issus. It was fought in 333 B.C., when Alexander was twenty-three, and was by far his greatest victory up to that time. The Persians lost heavily, and Darius, abandoning everything, fled in a rout.

One ancient historian reports that, in the middle of this battle of Issus, Alexander and Darius fought single-handed. Probably this did not really happen, although Alexander did have one encounter with a Persian in single combat, and got a serious wound on the thigh. If he and Darius had fought personally it would have been as if Churchill and Hitler had fought a duel to decide the course of World War II.

Alexander won at Issus largely by clever strategy. He put his right wing far forward, baiting the enemy.

Then, when the enemy's line became too extended, he moved with crushing force with his left wing, which the Persians had neglected. The terrific impact of the Macedonian phalanx won the day.

When the last Persian had fled, Alexander strode up to Darius' tent. He was overcome by the richness he saw— gold, precious ornaments, perfumes, and the like. He had never seen anything like this before. The Greek and Macedonian courts did not go in for such luxuries. He exclaimed aloud, almost enviously, "Darius is a king indeed!"

Alexander was tired and hot. He took off his armor, and asked where he could take a bath. The servants led him to the ornate golden tub which Darius used, and which was something worth coming miles to see. Alexander exclaimed boyishly, "I am going to have a bath in Darius' own bath!"

One of his respectful companions replied, even though he knew that his master *was* in many ways still a boy, "No, my Lord. It is now Alexander's bath."

Darius had fled in such hurried panic that he had even

deserted his queen, who was a pretty young woman, his mother, and two of his daughters, leaving them to their fates. These ladies, now prisoners of war, were brought before Alexander. Sitting next to him was his closest friend, Hephaestion.

Darius' mother, frightened and still confused by the events of the day and her son's abject defeat, thought that Hephaestion was Alexander and began to beg him for mercy. The mistake was natural enough, because Alexander and Hephaestion often wore identical clothes. A courtier explained her error, but Alexander cut in with the words, "It doesn't matter. Who speaks to Hephaestion speaks to me."

In those days female prisoners usually received very bad treatment from their captors. But Alexander behaved with the utmost civility and grace to the royal ladies. He allowed them to keep their magnificent jewels and to bury their dead with proper ceremonies.

He said to the pretty Queen, "You need not fear Alexander. I do not fight Darius. I fight merely for his kingdom."

If Alexander had any temptation to flirt with these queens and princesses, he resisted it. He declared, "It is more princely for a king to conquer himself than to overcome his enemies."

If—years later—he had followed this self-given advice, he might have had a different and much happier end.

During all this time, Alexander kept in steady touch with his mother, Olympias, to whom he sent regal gifts out of the loot of every battle, and with Aristotle, his great teacher.

Once he wrote to Aristotle, "I would rather excel in knowledge than in power." This was an attractive sentiment, if true. Also, he asked Aristotle to continue sending him books. Of all the rich booty Alexander got from Darius, one thing seemed to please him most. This was a small coffer studded with precious gems, and in it he put Aristotle's copy of the *Iliad,* which never left his side.

After the battle of Issus Alexander began to drink heavily for the first time. He needed some drug when he was inactive. Usually it was not the alcohol itself that he craved, but the talk that went with it. He loved to sit and talk all night. Plutarch records that when Alexander got drunk his talk became boring, which is what happens in the case of most drunken people.

Alexander still loved his friends and close associates. He wasn't spoiled—yet.

During a campaign in the Lebanon, one of his old tutors, Lysimachus, being old and slow, had fallen behind. Alexander generously stayed behind with him. Night came, and they saw campfires nearby, obviously enemy campfires. Alexander rushed to the closest fire, killed two men nearby, snatched a firebrand, and returned to his party. There they built a great fire, alarmed most of the Persians into running away, and fought off the rest.

After a period of rest Alexander marched farther down the Mediterranean coast (in what are today Israel and the Lebanon). He took everything in sight until he was stopped in his tracks at Tyre.

This great city, the mother city of Carthage, was—

and still is—a seaport, built on rocks out in the harbor. Because of its peculiar location, it was a difficult city to attack, and for the first time in his career Alexander was stumped. Not being able to reach Tyre, he tried to batter it into submission with catapults and flamethrowers. Finally he had to build a causeway over which his troops could travel from the mainland to the walls of the city in the harbor. Even so, the siege of Tyre lasted seven months.

Finally Tyre fell, and Alexander celebrated his victory barbarously. He sacked the city, burned it to the ground, and killed or sent off into slavery every man, woman, and child. He had done the same thing to Thebes—more or less. But Alexander never repented Tyre, as he repented Thebes.

Next, down the coast, he reached Gaza, which had been Samson's city. Gaza resisted him too, and there came another fiercely prolonged siege before the city fell.

This sea-route campaign was extremely important to Alexander, and strategically sound. He had to break the

Persian grip on sea power at all costs, because until he had complete command of the sea he was not safe on land.

Alexander was now just twenty-four years old. The whole world lay at his feet.

CHAPTER 11

EGYPT AND THE TEMPLE OF AMMON-RA

NOW ALEXANDER MARCHED INTO EGYPT. HE wanted to visit the site of the ancient Egyptian civilization that had helped give birth to man.

Egypt, which had been under Persian rule for 200 years, did not resist. In fact most Egyptians welcomed Alexander as a deliverer. They felt toward him much as the French felt about the British and Americans in 1945, when General Eisenhower pushed the Germans out and liberated Paris.

By this time Alexander was generally thought of not strictly as a Macedonian, but as a Greek. His forces were usually described as the "Greek" army. He encouraged this, because the word "Greek" signified something civilized and imposing. Furthermore, Greece and Macedonia had to all practical purposes become one country. In 332 B.C., as he entered Egypt, all the Greek city-states (except tough, reluctant Sparta) voted at last to accept him as their captain general, or supreme commander.

Alexander behaved generously in Egypt. There was no mass murder as after Tyre and Gaza. Maybe this was because the soft Egyptians did not resist. Maybe it was because Alexander felt ashamed of what he had done to Tyre, and was sick of blood.

One of the first things he did in Egypt, where he spent most of a year, was to found Alexandria, at the mouth of the Nile. This great city, which Alexander, of course, named for himself, is still one of the chief ports of the world.

Creating Alexandria was a remarkable accomplishment. Nowadays it might seem obvious that this was a good idea, but the Egyptians, in all their enormously long history, had never thought of it. Egypt had had a consecutive government for 3,000 years, which is a much longer span of time than from Alexander's day to this. Yet no one had ever dreamed of founding a city on this perfect strategic site, where the Nile and Mediterranean meet.

Alexander planned to build something on the model of Troy, and said somewhat boastfully, "Homer is going to be my architect."

It was necessary to mark out the site, but nobody could find any chalk. So Alexander ordered his men to procure some pale-colored grain, and drew the design with that. Then thousands of birds rose from the marshy Nile delta and ate the grain. Alexander was worried by this, but the soothsayers told him it was a sign the city would be a nurse and feeder of many nations. That satisfied him, and he ordered the workmen to go ahead with the building.

He had an amazingly creative imagination, and did better than just to copy Troy. He built the new city in the shape of a Macedonian cloak, square at the top, round at the bottom. When, finally, Alexandria was complete, it was by far the most impressive and best-laid-out capital in the world. It had straight streets, like those of modern cities, instead of bending, twisting lanes. The streets were numbered or lettered, as they are in New York or Washington, and they were the first in all history to have lights at night.

Then, at Aristotle's suggestion, Alexander sent down the Nile a scientific expedition that penetrated all the way into Ethiopia. The purposes of the expedition were to learn where the Nile rose, and what caused Egypt's abnormal rainfall and the fertility of the Nile valley.

Next Alexander journeyed into the desert to a remote oasis where he visited a famous shrine, known as the Temple of Zeus-Ammon. According to one theory, he took this difficult and perilous journey across the desert because of the bad omens at the building of Alexandria. More probably, he thought of it just as a new adventure. Alexander had great curiosity and wanted to see everything he could.

In the desert a great flight of crows appeared in the sky. Day after day they guided Alexander to the shrine. Legend even says that some crows circled far behind, to watch out for stragglers and help them catch up to the main column.

Even so, the tough Macedonian soldiery hated this trip, and grumbled openly. This is the first time that we have any record of dissatisfaction with Alexander on the part of his men.

At last Alexander reached the remote temple. He waited until the high priest, who was supposed to represent the Egyptian god Ammon, was ready to receive him. Alexander asked the high priest two questions—first, if all the murderers of his father Philip had been punished, and second, if it were really true that he, Alexander, was destined to conquer the entire world.

The priest answered "Yes" to both questions, and proceeded to disclose some secret oracles, straight from Ammon. One said that Alexander was not merely the son of Philip—or perhaps he was not the son of Philip at all—but of Zeus, or Jupiter. Hence, he was a god himself, born of gods.

This word spread like wildfire among the Macedonians, although Alexander himself did not take it too seriously at first. He said sensibly, "God is, of course, the Father of all men." He added, "Maybe He chooses the best to keep as His own."

But Alexander was shrewd enough to realize that, in oriental countries, the superstition that he was divine would be a big political and military asset. Also he remembered the various myths that had attended his birth, such as that his real father was a serpent.

For a time—publicly—he scoffed at the divinity legend. When he was wounded in battle, he pointed out the color of his blood, saying that it certainly looked like human blood, not something "divine." Nonetheless, the numerous people who wanted to flatter him and to gain his favor continued to talk about his "divinity." In time this began to influence him.

He wrote to Olympias that he had an important secret to tell her upon his return. Soon she heard what the secret was—people were saying that he was a god—and she laughed brutally.

CHAPTER 12

THE END OF THE KING OF KINGS

IT CAME TIME FOR ALEXANDER TO LEAVE Egypt, and to push on with his great task—the conquest of Persia. He had dallied long enough by the banks of the Nile, and he felt keenly the need for action, for refreshing himself with the heat of battle.

Darius knew this well and was scared. He had no relish for further fighting. Aware that he was no match for Alexander, he tried to make a truce with the Macedonians. Darius said that he would pay Alexander ten thousand talents, give him one of his daughters in marriage, and let him have all of Asia west of the Euphrates, if only Alexander would call off the war.

This was a princely offer. It promised a tremendous lot. Alexander called a council to discuss the matter, and the stout and wily Parmenio, much impressed, said, "If I were Alexander, I would accept this offer."

Alexander laughed. "So would I—if I were Parmenio!"

Like Grant in the Civil War and Roosevelt in World War II, Alexander insisted on unconditional surrender. He promised to treat Darius with courtesy if he surrendered unconditionally; otherwise, said Alexander, he would march against him and destroy him utterly, without mercy.

Then Darius got more bad news. His queen, Statira, who was still Alexander's prisoner, died in childbirth. Darius beat his head, anguished. It humiliated him terribly that Statira, so he thought, had died in dishonor. Emissaries promptly told him that, on the contrary, Alexander had continued to treat his Persian captives with extraordinary courtesy, and had given Statira a solemn official funeral. "There was no honor wanting at her death," Darius was informed. "Alexander is as merciful in victory as he is gallant in a fight."

Darius, deeply struck, then had a long discussion with Tiraeus, a member of the Queen's entourage who had managed to escape from the Macedonians. Tiraeus spoke of Alexander with the utmost respect and admiration, mentioning in particular his qualities of honesty, chastity, and nobleness of mind. Darius broke down and, holding up his hands to heaven, cried out that he was glad it was none other than Alexander who would succeed him, if indeed he were to lose his throne.

Meanwhile, Alexander advanced at the head of the men, whose morale was very high. They were eager to defeat the Persians once and for all. Everything went; the Euphrates fell to Alexander; he won easily what Darius had promised as a great concession.

To celebrate their victories, Alexander's troops devised a game, but soldiers, then and now, liked rough sports. One set of Alexander's men called themselves Greeks, while another pretended that they were Persians. Each team chose a champion, and these two men were symbolically called "Alexander" and "Darius." The two champions then fought a duel, first with their fists, then with stones and other weapons. Alexander and Philotas acted as seconds to the two contestants, and soon the whole army was watching the encounter. The man called Alexander won, and the real Alexander then rewarded him handsomely by giving him twelve Persian villages.

Finally the Greek and Persian armies approached one another and, on October 1, 331 B.C., they met at Gaugamela, near Arbela, in northeast Mesopotamia. This battle, usually called the Battle of Arbela, was one of the dozen decisive battles in world history. It marked the final collapse of Darius and his empire, and hence the end of Persian power in Asia. Not only did Alexander win; he won one of the most crushing victories in the history of war, even though Darius had sent a tremendous army against him.

Remarkable scenes took place the night before this battle. There was an eclipse of the moon, and Darius ceremonially paraded before his squadrons, inspecting them by torchlight. The Greeks, a few hundred yards away, saw the weird light of the flashing fires. Alexander held consultations with his soothsayers, then with his generals. They were stupefied by the number of men the Persians had massed against them, and also by the confused sound of voices that came out of the Persian camp like the roar of the ocean.

Parmenio made a quick suggestion—that Alexander should take advantage of the turmoil and attack at once, by night. Alexander drew himself up proudly and replied, "No. I will not steal victory."

He went to bed and slept soundly—so soundly, in fact, that Parmenio had to enter his tent the next morning and wake him, after having called him several times in vain. Parmenio asked him how he could dare to sleep so long, on the very dawn of what was bound to be his most important battle.

Alexander laughed. "But we have already won the battle!" By this he meant that Darius, in deciding to fight at last, had already destroyed himself. Darius, said Alexander, had simply saved the Greeks the trouble of chasing him any farther.

The next day Parmenio opened the engagement by attacking on the left wing, but he soon asked for reinforcements. Alexander did not like this. He sent a sharp message to Parmenio to die in his tracks rather than give an inch.

Then, putting on his jeweled helmet, Alexander donned his most magnificent armor. Thus garbed, he addressed the main body of his troops from horseback. As he raised his lance, he said that if it were really true that he was the son of Zeus, the Greeks were certain to win triumphantly. Then, he changed to Bucephalus, drew his best sword (a very light, well-tempered weapon, a gift from the King of the Citieians), and led the charge.

The Macedonian archers got busy overhead, the cavalry thundered along the flanks, and the phalanx moved into remorseless action. The Persians were hopelessly handicapped by a new artifice that they thought would be successful, but which did not work. They had attached scythes to the wheels of their chariots, hoping thus to cut down the advancing Greeks. But the scythe blades got tangled up, and soon the chariots could not move.

Darius himself was caught immovably in the middle of a seething traffic jam, while the horses plunged desperately, and piles of bodies mounted up. Finally he escaped, by fleeing on a loose mare. Needless to say, Alexander watched this mad spectacle with delight. The Persian resistance soon collapsed, and the battle became a rout.

After an interval there came the hot, wearying pursuit of Darius. King chased king. Alexander knew that the Persian ruler was finished as a practical force, but he wanted to capture him. The chase took many days. Then the Greeks found Darius dying in his chariot. He had been stabbed by his own men, who thought that they would have a better chance of getting away if they left the King of Kings behind.

Darius had just enough strength to ask for water, and

then cry out gallantly, "Thank Alexander for his courtesy to my wife and children. Embrace him for my sake!"

Alexander rode up a few minutes later, but Darius was already dead. Alexander cast his cloak over the body, announced that Darius' family would always be protected, and gave him a princely burial.

Later he captured Bessus, the Persian general whom he held to be responsible for Darius' death, and had him killed.

CHAPTER 13

INTO ASIA AND BEYOND

HALF THE EARTH WAS ALEXANDER'S NOW. HE was King of Macedon, King of Greece, King of Egypt, King of Persia, King of Asia. He was master of all sources of civilization on the planet, and he was only twenty-six years old. No record equal to this has ever been known to mankind.

Even today, the extent of Alexander's accomplishment rocks the imagination. In those days, around 330 B.C., his impact was even more staggering, and the romance of his conquests began to give rise to tales that are with us yet.

The driving motivation of Alexander's life was still practical. He wanted to travel, expand, and conquer. It never seemed to occur to him to wonder *why* he was doing all these things. As one modern commentator says, he was like a boy who cannot resist wanting to see what is beyond the next hill.

After Arbela he marched, explored, and fought for six solid years before he turned back. It is difficult to tell today whether there was any plan or design behind these turbulent, adventure-packed six years.

Naturally Alexander wanted to extend his empire to the farthest horizons possible; this was a perfectly legitimate ambition. Some historians think that, in addition, he was deliberately attempting to build up a new world order, uniting all peoples in a common brotherhood.

During these years, however, the tragedy of Alexander also began to take gradual shape. In the midst of glory, he sowed the seeds of his own collapse. After conquests such as no man had ever made before, he disintegrated. This gifted young man, so gracious and gallant on the great majority of occasions, gained practically all that he wanted, and then with crazy, selfish recklessness, threw it all away.

About his charm, there can be little doubt. Almost every surviving story about him—except those that show his tendency to be needlessly cruel when aroused—is proof of this point.

Out of these years, which carried Alexander to the crests of the Himalayas and the dank waters of the Indian Ocean, episodes and anecdotes pour with bewildering richness and variety. As for instance:

While Alexander was still hot on the heels of Darius, he had to cross a waterless desert. He and his men almost died of thirst. When they were nearly at the point of giving up, they ran into a group of wanderers who were mounted on mules, and carrying goatskins of water from a stream.

Recognizing Alexander, the leader quickly brought him a helmetful of water. Then the man explained that he and the others had gone out to find the water for their children, but they were glad to give it to him instead. If their children died they could still have more children, these nomads said; but if Alexander were lost, he could never be replaced. Alexander refused to touch a drop of the water, gave it back to the nomads, and marched on with his weary, thirsty men.

And:

Alexander decided to send back to Greece those of his men who were old or sick or crippled with wounds. An officer named Eurylochus managed to get his name on the list of these lucky ones to be repatriated. Then it was discovered that Eurylochus, who was not sick at all, had pretended to be ill so that he would not be separated from a girl, Telesippa, with whom he was very much in love. Telesippa was setting out for the coast, and Eurylochus wanted to accompany her.

Alexander told Eurylochus that he could not permit him to leave the army and return home under false pretenses. Also, since Telesippa was a free woman, Alexander could not order her to stay with the army. So he suggested that Eurylochus make Telesippa stay with him in Asia by the power of his own love—and that is what happened.

· · ·

After the collapse of the Persian armies Alexander marched down to Babylon and Susa. Here he found a gigantic fortune in loot, which the Persians had not had time to hide. In fact there was so much that, it is said, 10,000 pairs of mules and 5,000 camels could scarcely carry it. Altogether, at Susa and elsewhere, Alexander collected spoils that are estimated today to have been worth over two billion dollars!

Now, for the first time, Alexander penetrated into Persia itself. Heretofore, all fighting had taken place in buffer areas which, though under Persian control, were not part of Persia proper. He fooled the Persians by daring to march in winter, something unheard of, and reached Persepolis, Persia's richest city.

Fabulous revels and celebrations occurred for several days, and Alexander, putting a garland of flowers on his head, ordered his troops to set fire to Xerxes' palace at Persepolis.

At about this time, too, some of Alexander's men became discontented; it was the first time this had happened to any serious degree. They wanted to get back home. When the troops saw the palace burning, they cheered wildly at first, thinking that the fire was a signal for a return to Greece. They could not have been more wrong.

The only person who would attempt to control Alexander at this time was his mother, but she was far away. Olympias wrote her son regularly, and rebuked him on various occasions. She thought that he was spending too much money, and that his friends would take advantage of his generosity to betray him.

Alexander kept his mother's letters secret. He hated people to know that she was treating him as if he were still a mere boy. He always showed these letters to Hephaestion, but after one reading he put his seal on Hephaestion's lips, as if to emphasize the necessity for utter secrecy.

Antipater, his viceroy back in Greece, complained in one message about how Olympias was behaving. Alexander knew that he must be right, but he cried out,

"Little does Antipater know that one tear from my mother will wipe out ten thousand of his complaints!"

Alexander still kept in close touch with Aristotle, and, in fact, most of the worthy things he did in Asia, aside from winning battles, resulted from Aristotle's suggestions. He added scientists of all sorts to his entourage, an unusual thing to do in those days, and encouraged scientific research everywhere he went. He also kept a sharp lookout for phenomena in geography and natural history that would interest Aristotle so far away back home.

Alexander, himself, had an interest that occupied much more of his time and attention. This was the political management of the lands he had conquered. Shrewdly, he began to decentralize the huge Persian domains. Knowing that he could not govern all of it himself, he broke it up to a certain extent, and appointed Persians, as well as Greeks and Macedonians, to be provincial governors. One Persian official declared in amazed satisfaction, "There was only one Darius, but you now make many Alexanders!"

The richness of the Persian way of life, its idle luxuri-ousness, began to affect the Macedonians. They became soft, pleasure-seeking, and spoiled by too much loot. Alexander noticed that some of his companions began to wear extravagant clothes in the Oriental manner, and took to perfuming themselves. At this time he disap-proved strongly of such habits, though he was destined to do the same things himself before too long.

Sharply he rebuked one companion for dissipation, saying, "To live purely for pleasure is vile." Then, as if to strengthen himself against temptation, and to set an example, he went out of his way to prove that he was still as athletic, hardy, and disciplined as ever. He even fought a duel against a lion, which impressed a visiting delega-tion of Spartans mightily.

The amount of ground that Alexander covered is almost beyond belief. If we look at a map, we realize that even today such a trip would be almost impossible. Done overland on foot, the extent of his achievement can be better understood. To summarize and foreshorten this phase of his career briefly:

From Persepolis he went up to Ecbatana, along the spine of the Iranian plateau. Then he bent around to the northeast, touched on the shores of the Caspian, and sent an expedition out to map this huge, unknown body of water. He crossed the salt desert in what is now eastern Persia, and founded an Alexandria on the remote, desolate site of Herat. He progressed southward to Afghanistan and then took a side trip to the inaccessible mountains called the Hindu Kush. All this, it might be thought, would be enough.

It was not enough. He made a wild swoop north, cutting a circle in the land of the Bactrians and Scythians, until he reached Samarkand and Tashkent, which are now important cities in Uzbekistan. After founding the most distant of all the Alexandrias at a place now called Khudjand, in Tajikistan, he returned along the icy wall of the Himalayas to the Khyber Pass and India.

On the way into Parthia Bucephalus was captured by

savage tribesmen. But Alexander got him back, and then was so relieved to have the giant horse at his side again that he forgave and even rewarded those who had stolen him.

Now Alexander began to insist more seriously on being treated like a god. Deification, he found, appealed to the Oriental-minded Persians. Also he *liked* being thought of as divine, and he began to adopt the habit for which he had previously rebuked his men—that of wearing Oriental dress. But his men forgave him, because of his extraordinary personal valor in battle, for above everything else, he still loved to fight. Twice he was severely wounded.

Hephaestion continued to be his closest friend, but another companion, named Craterus, also became important. Alexander divided their functions cleverly, using the subtle Hephaestion to deal with the Persians, and Craterus, a much tougher character, to handle the old Greeks. Once he said, "Do you know the difference between Hephaestion and Craterus? Hephaestion loves Alexander, and Craterus loves the King!"

All this time, Alexander had to deal with pressing political problems. One was how to continue ruling his enormous and expanding territories while he was always on the march. Another was how to make the Greeks and Persians get along better together. He wanted to make the Greeks more like Persians and the Persians more like Greeks. To this end he chose 30,000 boys from all over Asia and had them trained under the Macedonian discipline.

Many of his own troops became so restless that he had to dispatch them home. By this time the army included a mixture of men from all over Alexander's empire. When he set out on the last lap of his journey, he had some 35,000 men. These he constantly stirred to greater efforts, saying that it was their duty to teach the barbarous Asiatics how to live.

CHAPTER 14

ROXANA, ALEXANDER'S WIFE, AND THE DEATH OF CLEITUS

IN BACTRIA, WHICH WAS JUST ABOUT AS remote as any spot in the world, Alexander captured Roxana, daughter of the ruling chieftain Oxyartes. From what accounts we have, it appears that Roxana was youthful and accomplished.

Up to this time Alexander had never paid much attention to women, no matter how attractive they might be. He had had too much on his mind to think about girls. But he fell in love with Roxana and offered her his hand.

He was now almost twenty-eight years old, and it was high time for him to have a queen.

Roxana, needless to say, accepted with pleasure this offer of marriage from the handsomest and most famous man in the world, and the ceremony duly took place. Alexander's devotion to Roxana appears to have been genuine. Still, as in the case of all great men of state, it is impossible to separate private from public motives. Marriage to a rich princess in Central Asia was a shrewd political device, and Alexander knew it. He wanted to do everything he could to encourage assimilation of the Asiatics he conquered, so that they would be easier to rule. Furthermore, Roxana's country had considerable importance strategically and politically.

Alexander's marriage seemed to portend happiness for himself, his queen, and his people, but then things began to go bad in other fields. He made grave mistakes, and in the end paid a full penalty for his hot temper and for the evil impulses that he either could not or would not control.

One of these impulses involved Philotas, the son of

Parmenio and one of Alexander's best friends since boyhood. Philotas was known as the most patient and valiant of all the Macedonians. But, spoiled by success and easy living, Philotas became vain and pompous, so much so that Parmenio had to plead with him to reform. Then, on what seems to be pretty flimsy evidence, Philotas was accused of taking part in a conspiracy to murder Alexander. There is no doubt that, influenced by a courtesan who betrayed him to Alexander, he had talked unwisely against his chief.

After Philotas was arrested and put to the torture, Alexander hid behind the curtains to hear what his former friend might disclose as he lay writhing on the rack. Philotas groaned pitiably, whereupon Alexander came forward and snapped at him, "You should not have such a faint heart, Philotas, if you go in for plots like this!" Then the unfortunate man was led away and executed.

This was horrible enough; what followed was even more horrible, and is the worst blot on Alexander's whole record so far. He knew that Parmenio, the father of Philotas, would go mad with grief upon hearing that

Philotas was dead. Parmenio had already lost two other sons in battle. Alexander sent emissaries to Parmenio, who was in camp behind the lines, and had this faithful old soldier assassinated before he could hear the news of Philotas' death.

Antipater, back in Macedonia, was so horrified by this outrage that he thought Alexander must have lost his mind. Men close to Alexander were frightened, too. The atmosphere became that of a witch hunt.

Then came the end of Cleitus, the brave officer who had saved Alexander's life in his first battle in Asia, on the banks of the Granicus, and who was his foster-brother. For years Cleitus had been one of Alexander's two or three most trusted friends.

Alexander, after a year in Bactria and its surroundings, still dallied in Samarkand. He was happy with Roxana, and if he felt bad conscience over Philotas and Parmenio, there is no record of it. Then, one night at a feast, he and Cleitus got drunk and had a savage quarrel.

Minstrels sang to the banqueting guests, a mixed company of Macedonians and Asiatics. One of the Asiatics started to make fun of the rough, tough, simple Macedonian soldiery, and Cleitus, feeling that Europeans ought not to be insulted in front of Orientals, rose to protest. Alexander replied by calling Cleitus a coward.

Cleitus became furious and reminded Alexander how he had saved his life. Also he pointed out angrily how much Macedonian blood had been shed to enhance Alexander's glory, and how the King had betrayed the Macedonian tradition by saying that Zeus, not Philip, was his father.

Alexander lost all control of himself at this, called Cleitus a villain, and accused him of stirring up rebellion among the Macedonians. With dignity Cleitus denied the accusation and added that the way Alexander was now playing up to the Asiatics made a sickening spectacle. The two men then began to fight.

Their friends tried to separate them, but it was too late. Enraged and heartbroken, Cleitus stood his ground. Alexander reached for his sword, but could not find it—somebody had taken it from him, in the hope of preventing bloodshed. Alexander then commanded the trumpeter to sound a general alarm, which the trumpeter courageously refused to do. Fellow officers thrust Cleitus out of the room, but, in a cold frenzy, he returned through another door, taunting Alexander with words from the Greek poet Euripides:

"Is it thus that Greece rewards her heroes?
>Shall one man claim the trophies
>Won by thousands?"

Alexander, wild with rage, then grabbed a spear from the nearest guard, and ran Cleitus through the body.

His remorse later was so extreme that he tried to kill himself. For three days he lay on the ground like a slave, sobbing. But his sobs did not bring Cleitus back.

Thereafter, as if he were punishing himself and at the same time punishing others for his own sins, Alexander's behavior steadily became more fierce and dissolute.

CHAPTER 15

ELEPHANTS AT THE GATES OF INDIA

AFTER COMING DOWN FROM CENTRAL ASIA and the rugged Afghan mountains, Alexander penetrated the Khyber Pass. In this almost totally inaccessible region, which only a handful of people ever see, the villagers today still try to sell coins and medals bearing Alexander's image. They say that these have lain there ever since Alexander first crashed through the Khyber Pass on the road to India, more than twenty-two hundred years ago.

On that journey, troubles began to thicken in the conqueror's path. A high member of the entourage was

Callisthenes, who was Aristotle's nephew-in-law and official historian to the expedition. Callisthenes, like Cleitus, fell out with Alexander. He too resented the King's Oriental dress and his demands that all, even the veteran Macedonians, should kneel and prostrate themselves when they came into his presence.

Publicly, Callisthenes refused to obey this demand, and Alexander became infuriated. Like Philotas, Callisthenes was then accused of conspiring against Alexander's life. Alexander did not quite dare to execute him right away, but packed him off to prison. One story is that Callisthenes met death by being eaten by lice, of which there were great numbers in the filthy Asiatic jails. Another is that Alexander waited a few months, until the Macedonians who sympathized with Callisthenes became quiet, and then had him hanged.

Alexander's army, though smaller than in former days, was unwieldy. This was partly on account of the immense spoils it kept on accumulating. Alexander made one of his quick, colorful decisions, of the kind that had made him such a hero to his men years before. He ordered his own carriage to be set on fire, as an example to the others, and the rank and file of soldiery cheered lustily.

He became more and more pitiless toward those who aroused his disfavor. One veteran Macedonian, Menander, was executed for having disobeyed a routine order. Omens began to be bad, and the soothsayers were in terror. But Alexander still thought that he could overcome any misfortune by the sheer force of his valor, his impetuosity, and his sense of the dramatic.

The early Alexander—of course he was still under thirty—sometimes shines forth again, as in this Nysa episode. But a rising tide of murder, corruption, and poisoned egotism was slowly, relentlessly, washing away his better self. When one Indian city resisted his advance, he put every living inhabitant to the sword, including the children.

Then, pushing forward, he encountered an Indian ruler named Taxiles, and again we see the old, attractive Alexander. This Taxiles was a prince of great shrewdness and nobility, and he won Alexander's respect by daring to talk back to him. Taxiles said, "Why should we fight? If I am richer than you, I will give you goods of mine. If you are richer than I, I will not scorn to accept goods of yours."

Alexander was delighted by this, took Taxiles off to a banquet, and got drunk. He made an alliance with him for the further conquest of India and gave him a large fortune in treasure. Alexander understood that bribes, disguised as gifts, were a good means of helping the spread of his empire. He was proved to be right when the news of his generosity spread through the region, and assisted his advance.

After his meeting with Taxiles, Alexander crossed the Indus and reached the river Hydaspes, which runs through what we call the Punjab today, in northwest India. A great Indian king named Porus rose to oppose him, and marshaled his forces on the opposite bank of the river.

Porus was a majestic figure, almost seven feet tall, and he gave the Macedonians, who thought by this time that they had seen everything, a new experience—he fought with elephants. These beasts startled Alexander's troops at first, but nothing could break the Macedonian discipline, not even armed elephants. It was not long before the phalanx was carving its way through the elephants exactly as it had carved its way through the Greek footmen at Chaeronea, or the charioteers of the King of Kings at Issus.

This battle with Porus, which took place in 326 B.C., was Alexander's last pitched battle of consequence. He won it by tactics now familiar. First, he made a daring crossing of the river at night. Then, holding some of his men back until the critical moment, he hurled his left wing irresistibly at the most vulnerable spot in the enemy lines.

Porus, mounted on a huge elephant and decked out in regal armor, became an easy target, and was struck by a dozen arrows. Nevertheless, he was able to ride off on his elephant after the battle.

Porus, suffering from his wounds, was taken prisoner and led up to Alexander. All of Alexander's gallantry rose again, if only because he was so impressed by the magnificent way Porus had handled himself. Alexander, feeling out the Indian ruler, asked how he would like to be treated. "Like a king!" responded Porus. Alexander then asked him what he meant by this. Porus replied, "Everything I mean is contained in that single word. I am a king."

Alexander, to his credit, then treated Porus as he deserved to be treated, in a kingly fashion, and Porus became his friend.

Bucephalus died of wounds received in this battle, and Alexander mourned him as if he had been human. A favorite dog of Alexander's, named Peritas, died at about the same time, and Alexander built and named a city for him, just as he did for Bucephalus.

CHAPTER 16

MUTINY

ALEXANDER'S MEN HAD NOW MARCHED about eleven thousand miles, and they had not seen their homes or wives in more than eight years. The battle against Porus was a victory, but in a way it was a defeat, for it broke the backs of the victors. India was too much for the exhausted Macedonians to take. In Plutarch's phrase, this great subcontinent "killed their hearts."

Alexander made shrewd use of Porus. By treating him kindly, Alexander had no trouble in controlling Porus' subjects. But elsewhere in India, in regions not controlled by Porus, Alexander had to keep on fighting. He subdued the people of fifteen different Indian nations—so the chroniclers say—and took no fewer than 5,000 towns and villages. Then he stopped. This was the last flick of the tiger's tail. The Macedonians were too exhausted to go farther.

Alexander had hoped to reach the Ganges, the sun-splashed river that cuts India in half. Instead he got only as far as the River Beas, quite a distance from the Ganges.

At this point his soldiers mutinied. It was a polite mutiny, but a mutiny nevertheless. The Macedonians bluntly refused to attempt to cross the Beas, or to continue the war in India. Alexander might have made an example of a few ringleaders, but it would have been of no use. The Macedonians had lost the will to fight, which means the end of any army.

Alexander tried to persuade his veteran heroes to change their minds, and resume fighting. Exhorting them, he stripped himself naked, and displayed his own wounds, saying that every different weapon known to man—sword, spear, battle-ax, arrow, dart—had left its scar on him. But the game was up. His men were deeply moved and respectful—despite everything, they still loved Alexander—but they refused to budge.

Alexander retired to his purple tent and, like Achilles, sulked there for days. His men, miserable at having to disobey him, clustered around the tent, making lamentations and pleading with him to accept their point of view. To them he was still incomparably the most fascinating man on earth, a leader-hero beyond compare.

Defiantly Alexander replied that, even if every single man deserted him, he would proceed through India *alone*. He promised his men everything—more spoils, more adventure, more glory to their names. He appealed vividly to their imaginations, holding up the glittering idea of explorations on the Caspian, the Indian Ocean, and even through the Mediterranean—westward—to Gibraltar, when the Indian campaign was done. But they still said "No."

Finally Alexander gave in. At last the Macedonian army turned around, having performed such prodigies as no other army has performed to this day, and the long march home began.

PART THREE

CHAPTER 17

THE RETURN

THE GREAT RETURN, THE LONG AND ARDUOUS return, was, in strict truth, a return—not a retreat. Alexander's men suffered horribly, but the experience was not like Napoleon's retreat from Moscow, or similar disasters. The Macedonians never broke ranks and never lost a battle.

Alexander, who had a keen sense of history, did his best before quitting the Ganges to leave his mark there for future generations to admire and venerate. The way he chose to do this was strange, and is a foretaste of how his mind broke up later. He caused armor, battle equipment, and apparel for horses, such as bits and saddles, to be made larger than the normal, and had great numbers of these scattered about. He wanted posterity to think that Alexander and his indomitable Macedonians were bigger than life-size.

He built a fleet and returned part way by boat, first on the Hydaspes where he had fought Porus, and then down the Indus, which separates India from Baluchistan and Pakistan today. He found travel by water refreshing and relaxing, but there came plenty of adventures on the way.

A warlike people, the Mallians, attempted to impede his passage. Their city had high walls, like Tyre, and was hard to attack. Alexander made some ladders and was the first man to climb up, mount the wall, and drop into the hostile city. So astounded were the Mallians by such daring that they thought Alexander in his bright armor to be a ghost. Scattering, they fled. Then they looked back, and saw that only two other Macedonians had joined Alexander in scaling the wall. So they fell on the three fiercely.

In the fighting, Alexander received a terrible wound in the breast, and then, as he fell, a Mallian stabbed him in the neck. As he collapsed, his two companions closed in around him to try to save his life.

Then, mustering every bit of his remaining strength, Alexander managed to rise and kill the nearest Mallian. By this time other Macedonians got over the wall and carried their gravely wounded king to safety.

Alexander almost died. An arrow had plunged into his chest, and its head, broken off, became lodged in the bone between his ribs. To get it out was a frightful job, and the pain almost killed him. For a long period he was too weak to move, and rumors spread that he had died. So he dragged himself out of bed painfully, got dressed in a nightshirt, and, to prove that he was still alive, showed himself to the troops who swarmed around the tent.

He recovered at last, and the voyage downstream was resumed. At one stopping point, famous all over India as a home of wisdom, he met ten philosophers. These men had been stirring up native revolts against Alexander. A judge was appointed, and it was announced that the philosophers who did not answer well would be put to death.

As his first question, Alexander asked one of the philosophers whether there were greater numbers of men dead or living in the universe. The philosopher replied, "The living, because the dead are no longer men."

He asked the second philosopher, "Does the earth or the sea produce more creatures?" The answer was, "The earth, because the sea is but a part of the earth."

Another question was, "Which came first, day or night?" The answer came, "The day, by a day." Alexander did not altogether understand this reply, but he commented amiably, "Strange questions necessarily produce strange answers."

He asked another of the philosophers, "How shall a man become beloved?" The philosopher replied, "He must be very powerful, without making himself too much feared."

Still another philosopher was asked, "How can a man become a god?" The philosopher was bold enough to answer, "It is impossible for a man to become a god."

Another question Alexander asked was, "Which is the stronger, life or death?" The answer came, "Life, because it has to endure much more than death."

Finally he asked the last philosopher, "How long should a man live?" The philosopher responded with a clever evasion, and Alexander laughed.

He was so pleased by this episode and by the manner of the philosophers that he decided to let all ten live, though the judge wanted to sentence them all to death.

Alexander's voyage down the rivers lasted seven months, and finally he reached the Sea Oceanus, which is the Indian Ocean today. He sacrificed to the gods and prayed aloud that no conqueror in history should ever go beyond the bounds of the great journey he had made. (Few men ever have.)

Now Alexander left India behind and turned toward home. He divided his forces, sending some on by boat, under a commander named Nearchus, through the Indian Ocean to the Persian Gulf.

He himself led the other contingent overland, across

the desert of the Mekran. This was the most punishing experience Alexander's army ever had. His men died like flies—of exhaustion, hunger, and above all thirst.

At last, half dead, the Macedonians reached a fertile area called Gedrosia. The people here were friendly and had plenty to eat and drink. In reaction from his ordeal in the desert, Alexander went almost berserk. He got drunk, feasted without interruption for seven days, and let his men run wild.

Soon Alexander, after founding and naming for himself a few more cities, approached Persia. He discovered that things were not going well there. He had been absent for too long.

Several of his provincial governors thought that he was dead, or would never return. So they had been looting the people. Persian satraps were fighting with the Greek and Macedonian officials, and whole provinces seethed with rebellion. Unrest and sedition had, in fact, spread all the way to Macedonia itself. Olympias had a favorite who, it seemed, ran off with the local treasury. Worse still, she and one of her daughters rose against

Antipater, Alexander's deputy, seeking to divide Macedonia between them.

In town after town, as Alexander marched on steadily, he rooted out the corrupt local governors, trying to restore order, bring relief to the people, get Greeks and Persians together again, and win confidence back.

Everywhere the countryside was impoverished, and the people hungry. In one locality the governor, thinking to placate Alexander, brought him three thousand talents, but no food or other provisions for his army. With icy contempt, Alexander fed the money to a horse. (The money was gold, not paper, and the horse couldn't eat it.) But everybody understood instantly what Alexander meant, and sought vainly to avoid his wrath.

Meantime Nearchus, Alexander's admiral, made a landfall on the Persian Gulf and plunged inland with a few companions to make contact with the main Greek body. Nearchus was utterly exhausted, and so ragged and unkempt that Alexander did not at first know who he was. When recognition came, Alexander embraced him. Then, thinking that the whole fleet must be lost, since

Nearchus had so few men with him, he burst into tears. However, Nearchus told him that the fleet was safe. Alexander wept again, this time from joy, and a tremendous celebration followed.

Now Alexander came to Persepolis, which he had left six years before. It was 324 B.C., and Alexander was all of thirty-two. The journey from India had taken a year and a half. Alexander visited the tomb of Cyrus the Great, the founder of the Persian Empire. The inscription on it moved and impressed him deeply: "O man, whatso thou art, and whencesoever thou comest, for I know thou shalt come: I am Cyrus that conquered the Empire of Persia, and I pray thee not to envy me for this little earth that covereth my bones."

Plutarch says that these words pierced Alexander's heart, and he stood there solemnly for a long interval meditating "on the uncertainty of worldly things."

At Susa something happened of evil augury to Alexander. An old Indian seer, by name Calanus, had been traveling with him. Apparently Calanus did not like what he, in some mystical way, felt might be impending. He had a funeral pyre built, said a cheerful good-bye to everybody, and set himself afire. As the flames roared over him, burning him to death, he never stirred hand or foot, or even twitched.

Alexander watched this spectacle, deeply moved, and then called for Hephaestion. He got ferociously drunk, and promised a crown of solid gold to whichever of his companions could drink the most. A man named Promachus won the crown, and died three days later as a result. No fewer than forty-one other Macedonians died too, following this debauch. Literally they drank themselves to death.

CHAPTER 18

ALEXANDER CONQUERS EVERYTHING EXCEPT HIMSELF

NOW BEGAN A KIND OF DEVIL DANCE, OR SO it seemed. Horror followed horror. Alexander's one-time magical charm, his fresh vitality, his extraordinary capacity to make people love and follow him without question—all these went. Instead he became a drunken wreck, and eventually turned into a maniac.

His army, which had once been as hard as steel, dedicated and devoted, became soft and stale. Its path became one of debauch, as Alexander's own evil habits spread to his followers. The stout Macedonians became almost as greedy and depraved as the worst of the Persians and other Orientals they had chased through Asia.

Still, Alexander held onto something. He always had interesting ideas. Nothing could destroy his originality, his capacity for dramatizing a situation.

Whether he thought of it consciously or not, one of his objects was to bring the world closer together. An obvious way to get started on this would be to mix up populations. So, having already married one Asiatic princess, Roxana, he now made a concrete example of his policy by marrying another, Statira, the daughter of Darius. (Years before, he had received her gallantly with her mother, after the Persian collapse at Issus.)

Some say that on the same day, during the same ceremony, he married another Persian princess, Parysatis, the daughter of Artaxerxes III. By this maneuver he bound himself—so he thought—to both wings of the Persian royal house, which were rivals.

He ordered a group of leading Macedonians to follow his lead and marry Persians, too. Then, in what must have been one of the most remarkable scenes the ancient city of Susa had ever witnessed, he set up and superintended the greatest marriage feast in history. No fewer than nine thousand of his men, Europeans, were commanded to marry Asiatic girls, in a single mass ceremony. Alexander gave a cup of gold to each bridegroom, and remitted all their debts. Ever since, this event has been known as the "Marriage of West and East."

The 30,000 Asiatic boys who were being given Macedonian training and Greek background were now summoned. The boys had developed into robust, well-disciplined young soldiers, and Alexander was delighted by the success of his experiment.

His Macedonian veterans were, however, far from pleased. They were jealous of these interlopers, and thought that their own influence would be lessened. Their suspicions seemed justified when Alexander picked a new bodyguard and made it exclusively Persian.

Hurt and angry, the Macedonians went to Alexander to protest, but he refused to see them. They waited outside his tent for three whole days, carrying no weapons and wearing shirts instead of uniforms, to show that they still remained loyal. On the fourth day Alexander came out of his tent at last, and the Macedonians called him their sovereign and master as always, while giving voice to their protest. Alexander wept—he seemed to be weeping a good deal these days—and said that he and the Macedonians would always be bound together. But the Persian bodyguard remained.

Alexander moved on to Ecbatana, in the kingdom of the Medes, and started drinking heavily again. Hephaestion, whom the King still loved above all men, fell sick of a fever. Unwisely he joined Alexander at a feast where he ate too much and drank an enormous quantity of wine. As a result he had a relapse and died.

Alexander went mad with grief—literally. He ordered the manes to be shaven off all the horses and mules in the army, as a sign of mourning. He ordered the battlements of nearby cities to be torn down, and commanded that, by terms of an oracle from Zeus-Ammon, people should worship Hephaestion as a hero.

Finally, in an outburst of pure savagery, as if he could forget the loss of his beloved friend only by drowning himself in blood, Alexander declared war against a harmless people called the Cossaeans.

Alexander's delusions of grandeur became more and more pronounced. A friend suggested that, to commemorate his fame, he should have his likeness carved on Mount Athos in Thrace. This would be hewn out of the living mountain, and would be so big that his left hand would house a city of 10,000 people, while from his right hand a river would be made to flow into the sea. Alexander reflected upon this tremendous project, and then rejected it on the ground that it was not grandiose enough.

By this time Alexander's old veterans, although they still loved him and still found it difficult to resist his charm, could no longer conceal their growing dissatisfaction. They hated the Oriental costumes and the way they had to prostrate themselves before their leader and kiss his feet as if he were the crudest kind of Asiatic despot.

Another thing that annoyed them was that Alexander had come to take with real seriousness the legend that he was a god, the son of Zeus. Men who dared to doubt this "fact," now official, were executed. The stout Macedonians knew, of course, that the claim to divinity was false, but they had to keep their mouths shut.

Unhappiness, dissatisfaction, and resentment seethed through the Macedonian army as Alexander proceeded up toward Babylon. The omens of the soothsayers were unfavorable, and for the first time in his life Alexander became really scared.

CHAPTER 19

THE DEATH OF ALEXANDER

ALEXANDER, LIKE ALL FRIGHTENED MEN, BE-came increasingly suspicious of everybody. He, who once held the trust of the world, now trusted no one. Nearchus warned him not to enter Babylon, and just as he approached the walls, a cloud of crows appeared in the sky fighting one another. This was considered to be a bad sign. So was another disconcerting event: when a beast was slaughtered for sacrifice, its liver was found to be missing. Then, to the mortification of all, a tame donkey engaged in combat with the best lion in Babylon, and killed it by kicking it to death. This seemed to show that nobody was safe, and that everything had become topsy-turvy.

Alexander, worried, seldom went into the town. Most of the time he lived on a houseboat moored nearby, where he was isolated and could be carefully protected. Steadily he became more uneasy, and had hysterics of remorse at some unworthy things he had done. His quarters were always full of whispering soothsayers now. These were the equivalent of his conscience, but they did not do him much good.

In particular he became suspicious of Antipater, whom he had not seen for eleven years, and who was still governing Greece in his stead. Antipater's son Cassander visited him, and Alexander behaved rudely to the young man. Cassander replied with clever poise; Alexander appeared to scoff, and said that such talk was the kind of thing people got from Aristotle, whom he now pretended to despise. The truth was that Aristotle had not forgiven him for having put Callisthenes to death.

Through one of his best oracles, Alexander heard from

the dead Hephaestion; he at once called for a feast to celebrate this extraordinary event.

On this occasion Alexander drank all night and all the next day. He caught cold as a result and complained of a pain between his shoulders as sharp as the wound of a spear. The cold developed into a severe fever which his body could not shake off.

Alexander's end was that of a man who, for good reasons or bad, had conquered almost the entire world, but who had never been able to conquer himself. The conquest of self is the greatest victory of all, but Alexander, even when he was at the height of his power, had never been able to achieve it.

His illness—probably it was a form of malaria, complicated by pneumonia—became more acute. Fever made him intermittently delirious. But on June 19, 323 B.C., he felt a little better (this man who had won so many fights against wounds and illness) and he ate some meat. This brought the fever back, but he was still able to get around to some extent. Nearchus visited him on June 20th and entertained him with tall stories about the Indian Ocean.

On the 21st Alexander was worse again, and his bed was moved outdoors so that he could get more air. He still had enough command of his faculties to tell his chief legionnaire not to let anybody visit him whom they did not trust.

Then, after another brief period of feeling better, his fever rose sharply again. On the 23rd he begged those closest to him, among the gallant band of old companions, not to leave his side, and slept fitfully. On the 25th, still burning with fever, he fell into a coma; his men thought that he was dead. A long parade of Macedonians crept mournfully by his bed, but traces of life still remained. Somebody asked him to whom his kingdom should go, and he summoned up his last strength to murmur faintly, "To the strongest!"

On June 28th Alexander died. He had reigned twelve and a half years and was not quite thirty-three years old.

Right to the end, Alexander's active mind overflowed with ambitions and ideas. He had plans for the conquest of Arabia, for irrigation projects in the Mesopotamian desert, for colonizing the Caspian area, for exploring the

North African coast, and for various other projects in political, scientific, and geographical fields. Apparently he never had the faintest idea that anything could ever kill him. He thought that he was immortal, and believed in his own destiny, above all. This is one reason why he never returned to Greece. He thought that he could go back to his Macedonian homeland any time. There was no hurry, Alexander felt.

Perhaps, if he had lived longer, a more cruel fate would have struck him. He might have gone into complete disintegration, and been forced to witness the loss or destruction of everything he had won, the collapse of all his triumphs. He was spared that humiliation.

CHAPTER 20

AFTERWARD

FOR A LONG TIME PEOPLE COULD NOT BELIEVE that Alexander was really dead. The challenge of his career was too great, his impact too enormous and profound. There was a long, angry dispute as to what to do with his body. A temporary resting place had been found for it, but he was not finally buried till years later, when interment took place at Alexandria.

Meanwhile terrible things happened. Olympias, thinking that her son must have been poisoned, put people to death right and left, including Iolas, the son of Antipater. Roxana had always hated Alexander's second wife, Statira, and at once had her murdered.

His son by Roxana was murdered too, and so was Roxana herself, who apparently loved Alexander very much. Another victim of assassination was a son of Alexander by another wife. Although this son bore the kingly name of Hercules, very little is known about him.

After these events, the empire fell to pieces. It is a high irony that Alexander's immediate successor, a general named Perdiccas, reached this post largely through the influence of Alexander's half-brother, Arrhidaeus, who was now a complete lunatic. It is even more striking, in a different way, that no fewer than five of Alexander's closest companions among the old Macedonians became kings. Such men as Ptolemy in Egypt and Seleucus in Central Asia succeeded him in various parts of the empire and founded dynasties, several of which lasted a long, long time. Alexander had always had the knack of picking good men.

Legends began to grow up about Alexander soon after his death, as if the bare bones of the truth were not enough. A romance of Alexander came into being, and was embroidered upon for century after century, all over Europe and Asia. However, no embroidery can ever be more magnificent than the simple outline of his career and conquests. No embroidery could be more tragic than the struggle between the richly gifted Alexander and the dark forces that eventually destroyed him.

There are plenty of black marks to be placed against Alexander, and the list of his cruelties is long. But he was certainly, beyond doubt, one of the most extraordinary young men who ever lived, and history can never forget him.

Whether or not he actually thought in terms of a world state, of the unity of all mankind as brothers under a single government, hardly matters. What does matter is that, whether he planned it that way or not, he did more to unify the known world than any human being who had ever lived.

Alexander was not merely a wrecker, a destroyer, like

some other conquerors. He had freshness, scope, and above all imagination. He brought Greek civilization to the entire East, which continues to remember him, for to this day, he is known everywhere in Asia as the great Iskander (Alexander). Also, he brought Asiatic civilization to the West. Not only did he serve to bring Europe to Asia; he brought Asia to Europe, too.

Alexander was part of an immense, inevitable historical process, and he left no real successor. But seeds he planted have been growing ever since. By opening up the world, by showing it to itself, he made possible the development of all manner of ideas.

As a result of his conquests most of the world came to know Greek ideas and culture, Greek books and philosophy, and the Greek attitude toward life. These spread out almost everywhere and still play an important role in our education and attitudes today. The paths Alexander carved between Asia and Europe stayed open forever after.

All this aside, the chronicle of Alexander's own brief life, his personal story, has stirred mankind ever since. He lived out a career which, in human terms, can never be matched or easily forgotten. Nothing will ever detract from the sheer romantic majesty of some of his exploits, or, despite all his faults, dim the great glory of his name.

Index

ABOUT THE AUTHOR

JOHN GUNTHER is best remembered for *Death Be Not Proud,* the bestselling story of the heartbreaking death of his son, Johnny. The book became a bestseller and was subsequently made into a movie.

John Gunther started writing seriously when he was in high school. He was attracted to history and politics and was literary editor of the college newspaper at the University of Chicago. Soon after graduating, he went to Europe as a correspondent for the Chicago *Daily News.* He worked in almost every country in Europe in the 1920s and 1930s and in 1936 he wrote *Inside Europe,* an extraordinary look at the culture and politics of Europe in the volatile years just prior to World War II.

His love of traveling took him to almost every country in the world. He later wrote a series of "Inside" books about Asia, Africa, South America and the United States. His extensive travels and his understanding of history and politics make him uniquely qualified to write about Alexander, the man who conquered the world.

BOOKS IN THIS SERIES

✳ STERLING POINT BOOKS